Forty years in Burma

J E. 1832-1915 Marks, W C. B. Purser

Forty Years in Burma

John E. Marks. ဆရာ.

စင်လိပ ဘုန်းတော်ကြီး ။

Forty Years in Burma

By Dr. *Marks*, with a Foreword by the Archbishop of Canterbury. Edited, with an Introduction and a Selection of the Author's Letters and Reports, by the Rev. W. C. B. Purser, M.A., Examining Chaplain to the Bishop of Rangoon ::

With Seventeen Illustrations,
including a Frontispiece in photogravure,
and a Map

NEW YORK:
E. P. DUTTON AND COMPANY
681, FIFTH AVENUE

Printed in Great Britain

FOREWORD

LAMBETH PALACE, S.E.

IT must be right that some Biography of Dr. Marks should be published. A man of remarkable personal powers, he had opportunities of an extraordinary sort, and he used them extraordinarily well. I imagine that the record of St. John's College, Rangoon, is in some respects unique among educational annals in the East, and the romantic elements in its story are as noteworthy as its consistent chronicle of steady work. The dominating personality of Dr. Marks deserves, and has here, I hope, secured, appropriate record. The missionary annals of our time would be incomplete without such a narrative in permanent form.

RANDALL CANTUAR.

Easter, 1917.

EDITORIAL

THE text of Dr. Marks' memoirs came to me in a somewhat confused state. It consisted of three documents. The first was made up of some articles published in one of the magazines of the Society for the Propagation of the Gospel in the year 1900 Dr. Marks concluded those articles by stating that he intended in the near future to publish in book form the story of his life. It is a great pity that he allowed this intention to be frustrated by his constant activity in deputation work on behalf of the Society. His health did not improve with advancing years, and it soon became obvious that in spite of the magnificent memory which he retained to the last, he no longer had physical strength sufficient to fulfil his original purpose

In this difficulty his devoted sister came to the rescue with the suggestion that she should write out at his dictation the story which he had to tell, so as to save him the fatigue of sitting up to a table. Increasing cardiac trouble had already caused his medical adviser to prohibit Dr. Marks from sitting at, or bending over, a writing table for any protracted period In this way the second document was produced It was intended, as far as I have been able to ascertain, to supplement at different points the original story which had already been published, so as to fill in details which had been previously omitted.

It has been very difficult to find out exactly the points at which this supplementary matter was intended to be fitted in, and I have only been able to do so by diligent reference to the diaries and reports which have been placed at my disposal.

The third document consisted of the recollections of Mr. David Marks, the only surviving brother, of his numerous and lengthy conversations with Dr. Marks. This document I have found of considerable assistance, especially with regard to Dr. Marks' reminiscences of King Thibaw and Queen Supayalat.

A narrative prepared in this manner cannot but betray traces of its composite character, especially as I have considered it my duty as editor to preserve the authenticity of the narrative at the expense of literary finish. There was a certain amount of redundancy in the narratives as they came into my hands, which I have tried to remedy ; but apart from that, the story as it stands is substantially as it came from the pen of Dr. Marks.

I have to acknowledge my indebtedness to the staff of the Society for the Propagation of the Gospel for the invaluable assistance which they have given me in my work. Dr. Marks' official reports to the Society have all been placed at my disposal, and I have been allowed to select from among the large number of photographs in the possession of the Society those which I considered of interest.

W. C. B. P.

Seaford.
    Feb 1917.

PREFACE

THIS book is written from no desire for mere personal advertisement, though necessarily it contains very much of my own personal adventures and experiences during my long residence in Burma.

It is the outcome of reiterated demands and urgent requests alike from personal friends and from those whom it has been my duty and privilege to address from the platform or pulpit during my visits to this country, and also, latterly, during my enforced stay at home on account of health, which prevented me returning to my residence and work in the East

I am well within the mark in saying that I have given more than a thousand such sermons, addresses and lectures, and I am unable to recall a single instance in which such an effort has not been received with deep interest and attention by my audience, whether consisting of ordinary congregations, of University and college assemblies, of Public or Private schools, or gatherings of children of all ages, or even of City merchants.

From nearly every one of these audiences a request has come to me that I should embody in book form the story in which my hearers have been so interested

Newspaper reports more or less accurate—generally the latter—only whetted this desire.

I have long felt that I ought to comply therewith, and have determined so to do, but my constant absence from home on deputation has afforded me very little leisure for such a task; and, moreover, I have delayed in the earnest hope that with renewed health and vigour, I might be permitted to overcome the scruples of the doctors and obtain their permission to pay a farewell visit to the country that I love so well, and there arrange in order the materials for this work Unhappily the decision of those to whose verdict I ought to bow has finally shattered the hope of my ever being able to return to Burma, and so I feel that now or never must be my motto if I would write my story

This, therefore, is the *raison d'être* of my book, which I now send forth with the trust and belief that the kind interest and indulgence which have ever been given to my spoken addresses, will be extended to my narrative in its present form.

I do not undervalue, nor seek to enter into competition with the many able writers—among whom I reckon some of my most valued personal friends—whose works on Burma, from various points of view, are before the public Necessarily, for the completion of this book, I must traverse much of the ground already covered by them, but I trust that there will be no unnecessary overlapping.

After all, the story which I have to tell is a personal one, and without undue egotism, I have constantly felt, and as constantly been assured by others, that it is the personal element which gives the greatest interest to such a narrative as mine, whether spoken or written. It is a story, not of what I have read or heard of, but of personal experience · of what I myself have done or tried to do, or in which I have participated.

J. E. M.

CONTENTS

ILLUSTRATIONS

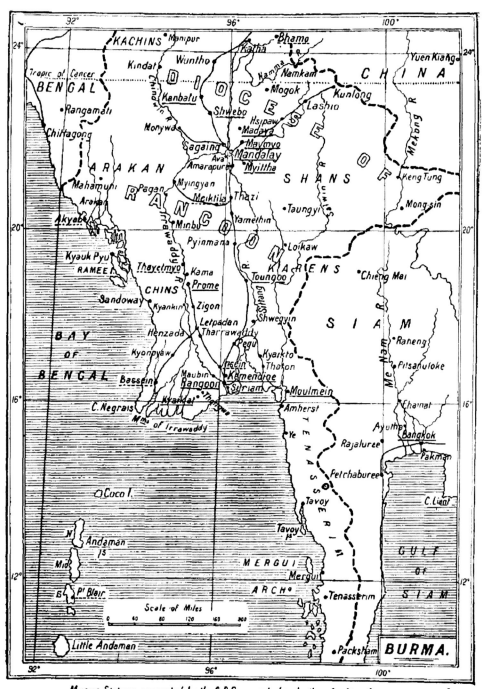

Mission Stations supported by the S.P.G. are underlined, other Anglican Stations ....

By kind permission of the Society for the Propagation of the Gospel in Foreign Parts.

[Facing p. 1.

Forty Years in Burma

INTRODUCTION

JOHN EBENEZER MARKS was born in London on the 4th of June, 1832. He was of Jewish extraction, and the remarkable vitality which, despite persistent ill-health, exacting work and a trying climate, enabled him to live a life of uninterrupted activity until the age of eighty-three, was doubtless an heritage from the hardy stock to which he belonged.

His early education was received at a school in the East End of London which has long since disappeared. He remained as an unpaid pupil teacher at the school in which he was educated until he received appointments successively at Wolverhampton, Birmingham and Evesham.

From Evesham he was invited by the Rev. T. O. Goodchild to become master of the

Hackney Free and Parochial Schools in Mare Street. His pupils were notorious for their roughness, and were locally known as the Hackney Bulldogs. He had desperate struggles with them, but his unique sympathy with boys, coupled with his genius for teaching, won the day, and the boys soon became attached to him.

After spending all the day in school, he used to devote his evenings to ragged-school work and evening classes for lads. In such work as this he gave material assistance to the parish of St. George's in the East, and also to Father Lowder.

He went out to Burma in 1859 as a layman for educational work in connection with the Society for the Propagation of the Gospel at the school which it had opened at Maulmein.

After working with great success for three years as a layman, he was accepted as a candidate for Ordination by Bishop Cotton of Calcutta, and was invited to undergo a special course of preparation at Bishop's College, Calcutta. He was there for a few months in 1863, and was ordained Deacon on All Saints' Day in Calcutta Cathedral. After a short

INTRODUCTION

furlough in England, necessitated by an attack of abscess on the liver, he was ordained Priest in Calcutta in 1866.

The story of his educational work in Maulmein, Mandalay and Rangoon is told at length in his memoirs, and it would be superfluous to tell it again here. The main facts are enumerated in the following resolution which was adopted by the S. P. G. on his death :

" It is with no ordinary feelings that the Society, assembled in its Monthly meeting in the Society's House on Friday, October 15th, 1915, places on the list of those who have departed this life the name of the Rev. Dr. J. E. Marks, assured that posterity will accord him a place among the great educational missionaries of this age. There are few also who have led a life so full of romance, and in situations which brought him into touch with some of the great political movements within the Empire. . . .

" Burma was the scene of his missionary labours, and he leaves a name in that land educationally, as great as that of Judson on the evangelistic side. In the region of romance there are few missionary episodes more fas-

cinating than the history of Dr. Marks' association with Mindôn Min and King Thibaw. The
former, though a non-Christian, built a church
and a school and a residence for Dr. Marks,
and sent the royal Princes to the school.

"But the monumental work of Dr. Marks
was the creation and development of St. John's
College, Rangoon, which, under his auspices,
became the leading educational establishment
in Burma. Not less than 15,000 pupils passed
through his hands, composed of almost every
nationality in the East. . . .

"He was presented with the Lambeth
Degree of D.D. in 1879 by Archbishop Tait,
in recognition of his eminent services to the
Church, and retired in 1900, but not to idle-
ness. Dr. Marks has been one of the most
indefatigable of helpers for the Society's cause,
and his presence had become known from one
end of the Kingdom to the other. The Society
never had a more devoted supporter, and is
proud of having had the name of this remarkable man and missionary on its lists."

The last fifteen years of his life were spent
in constant deputation work on behalf of the
Society, and during that period he must have

INTRODUCTION

preached in almost every Cathedral and important parish church in England. Failing health, aggravated by a motor accident, interfered with, but did not put a stop to, his activities. He was preaching constantly to within a few days of his death, and was actually engaged to preach in Chelmsford Cathedral on the Sunday after he passed away.

The story which Dr. Marks tells in the following pages needs supplementing in some respects if the character of the writer is to be properly understood. There were so many interesting events in Marks' life, that the reader is in danger of forgetting that the most interesting thing in the whole story is the writer himself. It is no exaggeration to say that for many years the personality of Dr. Marks was quite an important factor in Burmese life.

It was not so much his educational or missionary activity that secured him this prominence. It was the influence of his own personality. He had a perfect genius for forming and keeping friendships. Humble Eurasian orphans, Burmese and Indian schoolboys, and high Government officials were all attracted to him by his boundless affection, his open-handed generosity and his unstinted hospitality. His geniality broke down all the barriers of race, religion and social position, and won for him friends wherever he went.

Even his faults served to endear him to those with whom he had to deal. His impulsive nature compelled him to champion the cause of anyone who appealed to him for assistance, and in such cases he did not hesitate to tackle the highest in the land. He was often at fault in the causes which he championed, but the engaging frankness with which he acknowledged it often ended in drawing still more closely to himself the person whom he had attacked.

His account-keeping was the despair of his friends. He would give away his last rupee, and then wonder where on earth all his money had gone to. His generosity often got him into trouble with the authorities in charge of the finances of the Mission, and it was at last decided, on his own suggestion, to make one of his colleagues responsible for the keeping of the school accounts. But it was just this generosity and complete indifference to finan-

6

cial matters which endeared him to his numerous protégés.

During his residence at Mandalay, and afterwards at St. John's College, Rangoon, Marks kept open house. The hospitality of St. John's College was for many years a feature in the social life of Rangoon. From the Chief Commissioner downwards, civil and military officials, wealthy merchants, and all the leading lights of Rangoon society constantly accepted the hospitality which Marks so unstintingly offered.

It was not so much the good fare that was provided as the extraordinary genius for entertainment possessed by the host, which attracted his many visitors. Marks was a first-rate raconteur. His supply of anecdotes was limitless, and he narrated them with a quiet restraint which added immensely to their effect. Some of his stories were a little inclined to be Rabelaisian, and very much shocked those who expected missionaries to indulge in nothing but edifying conversation. But his missionary zeal was unquestioned even by those who would have liked to see it accompanied with a more puritanical spirit.

His hospitality and geniality did no harm to his missionary work ; rather, they attracted the assistance of many who otherwise would not have been disposed to sympathize with such objects.

No account of Marks' life would be complete which failed to give some information about his ability in this direction. Unfortunately the present writer is ill-equipped for the purpose, as he only met Dr. Marks on three several occasions. One such story must suffice, and that, alas ! will only be appreciated by those familiar with the Burmese language.

When I visited Dr. Marks on my first furlough, I was rather proud of my knowledge of Burmese, and tried, I suppose, to make an impression upon him. By way of testing me he suddenly asked : " What does *Nè nè ma sa hmin* mean ? " " It means, ' Don't eat a little,' " I replied. " No, it does not," said the Doctor. " It means, ' Eat a good lot.' I always used that expression when I went round the dining-room to inspect the boys at their meals."

My own translation was literal enough, but Burmese is pre-eminently a language of *double entendre*, and the interpretation put upon the words by the Doctor would certainly be the one which would be understood by the boys. At the same time, there would be sufficient trace of the opposite meaning for the boys to appreciate the joke.

It would be a great pity if the numerous stories which Dr. Marks used to tell in Burma were permanently lost. Perhaps one of his many friends will some day give us an account of his table-talk.

A word must be said here about Dr. Marks' relations with the high officers of the Government. From the time of Sir Arthur Phayre, the first Chief Commissioner of British Burma, until he finally left Rangoon, Marks was on terms of intimacy with the successive rulers of the Province. The first efforts of the Government to establish English schools had proved miserable failures for lack of the right kind of teachers. The High School in Rangoon had to be shut up for a time. Marks tells in his diary of a visit to the Government school at Prome. The pupils were all there, but there was no teacher, so he set about giving the boys their lesson himself.

Marks' astonishing success with the schools which he established attracted all the more attention because of the comparative failure of the Government in the same direction; and though the educational authorities were naturally a little jealous, the other officials constantly turned to Marks for advice on educational affairs, and showed their appreciation of his success by lavish grants in aid for his work.

Of all the successive Heads of the Province, Sir Charles Bernard seems to have been the one who was most intimate with Marks; and the little glimpses into the character of this magnificent administrator which the memoir gives us will serve to heighten the admiration in which he is already held by those who know Burma.

His successor, Sir Charles Crosthwaite, speaks of the heroic energy and devotion displayed by Sir Charles Bernard After the annexation of Upper Burma, Sir Charles Bernard had to administer the newly-acquired territory without adequate machinery, in addition to bearing his previous burden of governing the Lower Province. The Upper Burma Secretariat was at Mandalay. "When Sir Charles was in Rangoon, he relied to a great extent on his memory. Letters and telegrams received from Mandalay were dealt with and returned with his orders, no copies for reference being kept." Anyone familiar with the work of the Administration of India will realize what an intolerable burden Sir Charles Bernard was attempting to carry.

His relations with Dr. Marks confirm the impression left on our minds by the above quotation of the tremendous energy of Sir Charles Bernard. When Marks was suffering from one of his periodic attacks of ill-health, the Chief Commissioner came personally to visit him in his little room at St. John's College, and carried him off to Government House. During the last Burmese war Sir Charles copied out all the official *communiqués*, as they were received from the field force, with his own hand, and sent them to Marks at St. John's College.

This series of notes terminated with the following laconic communication, dated Government House, Rangoon, December 2nd, 1885 : " There seems a chance of your soon

seeing your long-lost and much-cherished pupil.
Ex-King Thibaw was to-day at Minhla on
board the *Thooria* on his way down the river.
I can't help feeling some sympathy for the
poor creature in the plight to which he has
come.—Yours sincerely, C. BERNARD."

Was it desirable that a missionary, engaged
in the propagation of his own particular religious opinions, should be on terms of such
intimacy with Government officials, whose
supreme duty it was to administer the Province
with absolute impartiality, and without showing any favour to any religious body ?

The question is one of perennial interest in
India, where a professedly Christian Government has to administer the affairs of people
who are for the most part non-Christian.
Shall the Government show preferential treatment to Christian or non-Christian institutions ? In the past, the Government has
answered this question by asking another :
Which kind of institution is the more efficient ?
In Marks' time it was the Christian institution
which was demonstrably the more efficient,
and which received preferential treatment from
Sir Charles Bernard and other wise rulers.

INTRODUCTION

But in the future this is by no means likely to be the case, and if missionaries should be inclined to lament the change, they will find much in Dr. Marks' memoirs which will tend to console them.

The favours shown to Marks by King Mindôn did little to encourage the spread of Christianity in Mandalay. The help given by Government to St. John's College, while it enabled it to develop into an important educational foundation, did not succeed, in any appreciable measure, in commending Christianity to the Burmese. Dr. Marks' experience tends to prove that Government patronage can do no more now than it did in the time of Constantine to inculcate essential Christianity.

Marks did not lose his power of making and keeping friends after his retirement from active service in Burma. Many will recall the hospitality dispensed by his sister at their house in Croydon, especially the gatherings which took place annually on the Doctor's birthday. The event was made the occasion for the reunion of friends old and new, and became—what he called his house—a veritable " Burma " in England.

FORTY YEARS IN BURMA

All who were privileged to enjoy the hospitality of the Croydon " Burma " will recall the way in which the Doctor beamed round on his guests ; how untiring he was in relating stories of his work in Burma ; how naive was the pleasure with which he displayed the magnificent rubies and other jewels which had been presented to him by King Mindôn and his numerous Burmese pupils and friends. He showed himself there in his true character as the most genial, the most entertaining, the most generous of egoists !

There remain three aspects of Marks' work which must be dealt with at some little length in order that the reader may understand and appreciate the significance of the story which he tells. These are : (1) His relations with King Mindôn ; (2) his work as an educationalist ; (3) his connection with public affairs.

Dr. Marks and King Mindôn*

There is no doubt that the most romantic part of Dr. Marks' life was the period 1868–1874, which was spent in Mandalay, and during which he experienced, in varying

* cf. The whole series of letters in the Appendix.

degrees, the patronage of the King of Burma. It is important to realize that Dr. Marks was not the only Christian Priest to enjoy that fickle monarch's friendship. As he himself points out, the Roman Catholic Priest and the Armenian Bishop were both receiving help from the King before his own arrival in Mandalay.

It will help the reader to understand the true position of things if I quote the Roman Catholic version of the matter as set down by that most distinguished Prelate, Dr. Bigandet, in his book, " A History of the Catholic Burmese Mission."

" When the Bishop was in Mandalay in 1859, the King urgently pressed him to give him the Rev. Father Lecomte for the education of his children and those of his brother, the heir-apparent. The request was granted, though with a certain amount of reluctance, based upon the little hope entertained of the realization of the plan.

" Father Lecomte came to Rangoon to purchase what was necessary for the future establishment, and after completing his purchases, he returned to Mandalay in all haste.

But the mind of the King had already under-gone some changes, owing to the influence of the *Hpôngyis*, and perhaps of the women of the Palace. He would send to the school only some of the boys who were loitering day and night in the Palace. As the missionary had positive orders not to hold a school except for the benefit of the King's sons, he declined His Majesty's offer.

"In 1867 His Majesty placed under the charge of Father Lecomte twelve or fourteen boys belonging to some officers of the Palace. The boys were to learn the English language and the rudiments of those sciences which are taught in European schools. The excellent father has devoted himself to that task with great zeal and courage, and has succeeded as well as it was possible with boys of that country.

"Ever since his accession to the throne in 1852, King Mindôn has shown a real dis-position to help the missionary residing in the royal city. Father Abbona had known him well before his accession to the throne. He was fond of conversations on religion, and appeared much pleased with hearing particulars concerning the creed of the foreigners—*i.e.*, the Catholics.

" But this fondness was with him, as with all Burmese, the offspring of mere curiosity, and that even of a very superficial kind. Before His Majesty's mind was so much taken up with mercantile speculations, the writer often had the opportunity of discussing religious matters with him ; but he soon found that the King looked upon such discussions as matters of amusement, or, at the most, intended them merely to make a display of his knowledge of the Buddhist books, and particularly of the metaphysical parts of them. Never has he exhibited, even for a moment, the least inclination to reflect upon the capital truths fundamental to every rational being, viz., God, Creation, Providence, etc. With a childish sneer he laughed at the idea of a creating power, and now that his mind is entirely engrossed with the gains and profits which he desires to make, he cares no longer for religious topics.

" It may be, too, that he has found it impossible to maintain his footing in carrying on a fair discussion, and that he has given it up in despair. Certain it is that, notwithstanding what has been asserted to the contrary by persons who ought to know better, the King has never had the remotest idea of studying carefully and seriously the tenets of Christianity, and that he has always been a staunch and fervent supporter of Buddhism. Is he led to this line of conduct by political motives ? Does he hope thereby to obtain a greater and stronger influence over his people ? I believe that his acute and cunning mind can easily reach so far and make religion a means to carry out his plans.

" Be that as it may, it is certain that he has been liberal in assisting the Mission of Upper Burma When the Capital was transferred from Amarapoora to the present site of Mandalay, the King gave a fine piece of land, both for the church and the dwelling of the missionary, and bore almost all the expense of building the house. Whenever the Bishop has visited the city, the King has liberally given him money to defray his travelling expenses.

" The writer is delighted herein to acknowledge the many tokens of kindness which the

INTRODUCTION

King has conferred upon the Catholic Mission. But, at the same time, to avoid misunderstanding, it ought to be admitted that the liberality of the King extends also to the ministers of other denominations, though to different degrees. *He has lately contributed most liberally in setting up a school and a church for an English minister belonging to the Protestant association for the propagation of the Gospel. It is true that the said minister was backed by the powerful and active influence of the Chief Commissioner of British Burma, as well as by the incessant interference of the English Resident at the Court of Mandalay.* The King, as a true and clever politician, never does anything without expecting some return in one way or another. By favouring the English minister he expects to ingratiate himself with the English Governor, and hopes to find in his protégé an individual who, in case of difficulty arising, will be able to lend him important support.

" Moreover, the King, in the kindness which he vouchsafes to foreign ministers of religion, is influenced to a great extent by an ill-disguised vanity and a love of having his

name honourably mentioned *et late et circum,*
with praises and acclamations for his incomparable generosity.

"After the death of the Crown Prince and
the almost total destruction of his family,
followed by the revolt of his two sons, the
King grew fearful and timorous. He thought
his position fraught with perils and dangers.
Thence his settled idea of concentrating all
the power in his own hands. Contrary to
the immemorial custom of having always a
member of the royal family designated heir-
apparent, with a suitable amount of power,
influence and retinue, the King would never
allow one of his sons to be designated as his
successor. He feared lest he might plot against
him and hurl him from his throne.

"The head of the Buddhist religion, called
the *Thathana-baing,* happened to die two years
after the heir-apparent, but the King would
not suffer another to be appointed in his
stead.

"He told the writer, in the course of one
conversation, that he himself, assisted by four
dignitaries, would manage all the affairs of a
religious character. He is a true Czar in his

dominions. His greed of influence and power is so great, that he wishes to be the only trader in his dominions, and the only man who has a right to grasp profits. But withal he is not a miser. He is fond of money, but not for the sake of hoarding it as his predecessors did. He wished to have it to spend it as he liked.

" His Majesty did all in his power to induce the writer to fix his residence in the Capital. He promised him a monthly allowance for personal support. He gave him a very fine and extensive piece of ground whereupon a spacious brick building was erected for his residence. The writer expressed to the King his grateful acknowledgments for this act of kindness. He took possession of the place, but never dwelt therein. He devoted the building for a school, and up to this day it has been used for that purpose."

I have taken the liberty of quoting Bishop Bigandet at such length because his book is not easily accessible to the general public, because of the high authority of any statement made by so careful and profound a student of Burmese affairs, and because of the light

thrown by this particular statement upon
the relationship which existed between Dr.
Marks and Mindôn Mın. It is important to
remember that Dr. Marks was not the first,
much less the only, missionary who enjoyed
the Burmese King's favour.

The whole episode appears to be nothing
less than a deliberate, ıf somewhat childish,
plot on the part of King Mindôn. He was well
aware of the powers of the priesthood. He
fully comprehended the influence wielded by
the Buddhist monastic order from the *Thathana-
baing* down to the humblest novice, and, as
is indicated ın the above quotation, he had
deliberately exploited that ınfluence for his
own purposes. Could he not influence the
French and British Governments through the
French Roman Catholics and the English
missionaries ?

Dr. Bigandet was in a far more difficult
position than Dr. Marks, for what the King
expected of him was to connive at, perhaps
even aid and abet, a treasonable agitation
against the British Government. Those were
the days when the French and the English
were rivals, and when it was still undecided

as to which should be the paramount Power in Upper Burma. It is greatly to the credit both of the wisdom and the integrity of the good Bishop that he immediately perceived this and refused to become the King's agent.

Dr. Marks well knew what the King expected of him, and set himself from the very first against allowing the King to exploit his influence with the Government. He knew that he took grave risks of compromising himself by accepting the King's bounty, but he trusted to his own transparent *bona fides* to save himself from the difficulties that might arise. In his zeal for missionary education he was prepared to face the risks involved in being the protégé of a Buddhist monarch, but the position was an impossible one from the first. The King was alternately gracious and overbearing, according as he approximated to the realization of his ambitions. Time and again only Dr. Marks' extraordinary tact and ready wit saved him from forfeiting the royal favour.

It must be remembered that in those days Burma was in the Metropolitical See, so that Dr. Marks' Diocesan was the Bishop of Calcutta. It was through him that the King

hoped to influence the Viceroy, and to get back
once more into his own hands the Provinces
which had been annexed by England. Dr.
Marks' memoir and his letters clearly indicate
the eagerness with which the King looked forward to the visit of Bishop Milman to Mandalay for the consecration of the church,
and the disgust which he showed when he
found that the Bishop had returned to Calcutta without even granting him an interview.
He took care that this should not happen on
the Bishop's second visit.

The Bishop went to the Palace with Dr.
Marks and was graciously received, but when
he steadily refused to be drawn into any conversation about political matters, the King,
realizing that his ambitions in that quarter
were doomed to disappointment, showed his
disgust by bringing the interview to an abrupt
conclusion We are told by Dr. Marks that
the King's sons *never again attended school
after the Bishop's first visit to Mandalay.*

The King did not immediately withdraw
his support to Dr. Marks, but there is no doubt
that his favours were bestowed more and
more grudgingly ; and after experiencing all

the bitterness of those who put their trust in princes, Dr. Marks was at length recalled from Mandalay.

DR. MARKS AS AN EDUCATIONALIST

From first to last Marks' work in Burma was educational. Although he came out to Burma as a missionary, he definitely took the position, from the very outset, that the Burmese could only be influenced by Christianity through educational work. Christianity, as a religion, provoked the Burman to nothing more useful than barren controversy. But Christianity as English custom inspired him with all the respect which he paid to the British civil and military administration. Hence Dr. Marks' lifelong work in establishing English missionary schools all over the country.

In attempting to appraise the value of such work, it must not be forgotten that those were early days, and that Dr. Marks was a pioneer. Some of the schools which he established have disappeared. Some of the principles for which he contended, as, *e.g.*, the co-education of Europeans and Burmans, have

been definitely decided against him. Many of
the questions which agitated him and his contemporaries no longer awaken any enthusiasm
one side or the other. Has Dr. Marks, then,
any right to be considered an educationalist
in any real sense ?

To anyone who knows Burma it would be a
sufficient answer to this question to point to
St. John's College and other smaller educational institutions up and down the country
which remain as permanent results of his work.
But I do not think that we of a later generation can do credit to his work without reference
to one of his contemporaries. I therefore
take the liberty of quoting in full a letter
written to Dr. Marks by Sir John Jardine
in 1913.

Sir John says : " I write to announce the
coming of an event which you have long
desired, I mean the establishment of a University at Rangoon. In reply to a recent
question of mine in the House of Commons,
I was informed that although details have
not been settled, the Government of India are
making provision of funds for the establishment of the University.

Pupils and Staff of St. John's College, Rangoon.

[Facing p. 26.

INTRODUCTION

" You will remember that some of us in the very early days of the Educational Syndicate had a vision that this was to come, and that we did our work in anticipation thereof, keeping debates on a high level, providing a library, honouring scholars and scholarship both European and Oriental, protecting and super-intending teachers, creating public opinion, trusting the people and winning public confidence, fixing standards of all sorts, making examinations in all kinds of learning, and enlarging jurisdiction in spite of some opposition of officials.

" Apparently we laid the foundations well ; the Syndicate has lasted till now, and soon, I hope, will be merged in the greater institution. Not many of our colleagues, perhaps, looked so far ahead. Bishop Bigandet did, but he has passed away before seeing the University he wished for come into being. You are a survivor ; a generation has passed away; but I write in fullness of heart to you, as I shall never forget how thoroughly you worked in this great cause, and how constantly and warmly you supported our early efforts in the spirit in which Sir Charles Ber-

27

nard created and trusted that important Board.

" You and I had to frame a policy and to fight for it, and to spend many weary hours over it. I hope that our labours and honest hopes have been blessed, and that we have done something for the public welfare and in the spirit of the Author of our Faith."

No higher praise of Dr. Marks' educational work could be desired than this, and there are few who can speak with greater authority on the subject than Sir John Jardine. The Educational Syndicate referred to by Sir John was an attempt to co-ordinate the various societies interested in educational work in the country, and, in spite of all its obvious defects, it has been of inestimable service to the cause of education in Burma. That success has been due in large measure to the enthusiasm of the early members, and though Dr. Marks is by no means the only one of these who is entitled to praise, his claim must not be overlooked.

Marks was too strong a personality to work harmoniously on a Board with others. As he himself has told us, he was strongly in favour

of a committee of one, and if he fell into dis-
favour in later years with the educational
authorities in Burma, it must be attributed
rather to this defect in his character than to
a deficiency in his educational principles.

It is not, however, as an educationalist, in
the wider sense, that Dr. Marks can lay claim
to distinction. It was rather in the more
restricted sense as a schoolmaster that his work
commends itself to us. His genius in this
direction is unquestioned. As early as 1861,
when he had only been little over twelve
months in the country, it was already recognized by his colleagues. The Chaplain of
Maulmein in his report to the S. P. G. stated
that Mr. Marks was a first-rate schoolmaster,
zealous and most fond of his particular work,
and that " He has such a happy way with him
in the treatment and management of boys,
that they soon become strongly attached to
him, and his personal influence is very great."

The writer of this report succinctly states at
the very outset of his career what was the
secret of Dr. Marks' success. It was due, not
to his knowledge of high educational principles, or of extraordinary powers of organiza-

tion. It was due simply to the power of his own personality.

He had a passionate love for boys and an extraordinary way of winning their affection. He was ready to give anything in his power to help his " sons," as he affectionately called his pupils. His time, his money, his health, were all given without stint for their welfare. In the diaries there are frequent entries like the following :

" 29-1-69. Having sat up all night with Kyay Hmin, who for a long time was delirious, I slept a little this morning."

" 30-1-69. Went to bed at 4.30 a.m. Up at 8.30."

These are just little indications of what all his old boys say, that he would sit up night after night with sick boys, and yet go on quite cheerfully with his teaching work the next day.

There is another entry in the diaries, on June 21st, 1869, about the time of the opening of the Royal School at Mandalay, which again illustrates the affection which he had for his pupils : " Give me, O Father, wisdom and earnestness to work for Thee and Thy glory in teaching these dear boys. Bring them to the Good Shepherd of their souls and keep them as Thine, now and ever."

It is not to be wondered at that affection shown in so real and practical a form was reciprocated by his Burmese and Eurasian pupils. Devotion to " The Doctor " amounted almost to a cult, which, after his retirement from active service in Burma, showed itself in the formation of the " Marks' Memorial Fund."

Two little incidents will serve to illustrate the relations which existed between Marks and his pupils. The first is told by the writer of the obituary notice in the *Rangoon Gazette*. It was on the eve of Marks' return to England after his last visit to Burma. All his packing had been done, and he was to go on board the following day. He had been desperately ill, and was only allowed to see privileged visitors. One of these, on saying good-bye, ventured to ask him how his finances stood. " After a brief spell the truth came out : the sum that had been put aside for personal expenses had gone ; it had been given to a Burman protégé who had come to him with a tale of domestic distress." One solitary rupee remained to carry him back to England !

The other story was told me in Rangoon by one of the staff of St. John's College. In the early days of that institution some of the teachers were returning from Rangoon in the small hours of the morning after a somewhat riotous evening. They had been coming along the road in a very noisy manner, until one of them suddenly recognized in the distance the little tiny room which for many years served the " Doctor " as bedroom and sitting-room. He at once put up his hand and said : " Hush, the *Hpôngyi !* " There was immediate silence, and all of the party, Eurasians and Burmese, sat down solemnly in the road and took off their boots before entering the compound, just as they would have done if they had been going into a Buddhist monastery, and then proceeded silently to bed.

Marks tell us in his memoir that his educational text-book was " Tom Brown's School Days." Dr. Arnold, of Rugby, was the model upon which he tried to fashion himself. It must have been of very great interest to him to find that his first Bishop, Dr. Cotton of Calcutta, was the " New Master " of that great book. If Arnold's system was founded on the establishment of a relationship of mutual affection and regard between master and pupil, then it can be affirmed without any danger of contradiction that Marks was successful in introducing that system into the schools which he founded in Burma.

Allusion has been made above to the foundation of the "Marks' Memorial Fund." It began its existence in 1898, when Marks retired from active work in Burma. It was virtually an old boys' club, of which the members were the "sons" of Dr. Marks whom he had educated at one or other of the schools which he had founded. But the fund was founded, not primarily for the encouragement of *esprit de corps* in St. John's College, though that undoubtedly was one of the results of its establishment, but for the provision of a pension for their superannuated principal.

Gratitude is not a virtue which is very prominent in the Eastern character. In fact, most Englishmen who have spent their lives and given their best years to the amelioration of the lot of their fellow-subjects in India, frequently complain that their work is but little appreciated by those who have chiefly bene-

fited from it. They are " as the remembrance
of a guest that tarrieth but for a day."

Dr. Marks had no such experience. He was
remembered by his " sons " to his dying day,
and the gratitude of those whom he had
worked for was shown, not in empty expres-
sions of regard, but in the practical form of
a pension fund. The fund was sustained all
the seventeen years which lapsed between
Marks' retirement and his death, and the
affection which prompted it was demonstrated
by the fact that it included a constant supply
of the cheroots for which Burma is famous,
and which the Doctor never lost his liking for.
The " Marks' Memorial Fund " did not cease
even with his death. It is still maintained,
and the proceeds are being devoted to the
erection of a memorial chapel in connection
with St. John's College, and to the foundation
of scholarships for poor Burmese students.

Dr. Marks and Public Affairs

Dr. Marks took a lifelong interest in public
affairs, especially during his residence in Rangoon. When the atrocities in Upper Burma

were perpetrated by King Thibaw, it was a letter from his pen to the Rangoon press which first called for the vigorous protest which was expressed in a magnificent mass meeting in Rangoon, at which he was one of the speakers, and which ended in the intervention of the British Government.

But it was mainly in connection with the volunteer movement and with the Rangoon Municipality that his activities in this direction manifested themselves. How far it is desirable for an educational missionary to take an active part in such affairs is a matter of opinion, and, unfortunately, Dr. Marks did not always see eye to eye with his colleagues on this point. Bishop Strachan considered it his duty to make a protest, and it was one of the causes for the strained relations which existed for a long time between these two zealous missionaries.

His activities in connection with the volunteer movement were less open to question, and in this, as in so many other matters, Marks was the pioneer in Burma. St. John's College Cadet Corps was the first volunteer detachment connected with any school in Burma.

For many years it enjoyed the reputation of being the most efficient of all the volunteer corps in the Province. During the last Burmese war all the members, with a few insignificant exceptions, volunteered for active service, and though Sir Harry Prendergast did not see his way clear to accept the offer, the corps was placed under active service conditions, and became, for the time being, part of the garrison of Rangoon.

Since that time several other schools in Burma have started cadet corps, and the movement has passed beyond the experimental stage. It is certain to become more and more important in the future as the duty of national service for all the citizens of the British Empire becomes more clearly recognized. During the present war many of the various races of Burma have asked for permission to serve in the British army, and although the authorities naturally hesitate to enrol all the men of fighting age, or to put arms in the hands of those who might misuse them, there seems little to be said against, and much to be said in favour of, training to arms the small minority of students who have had the advantage of an

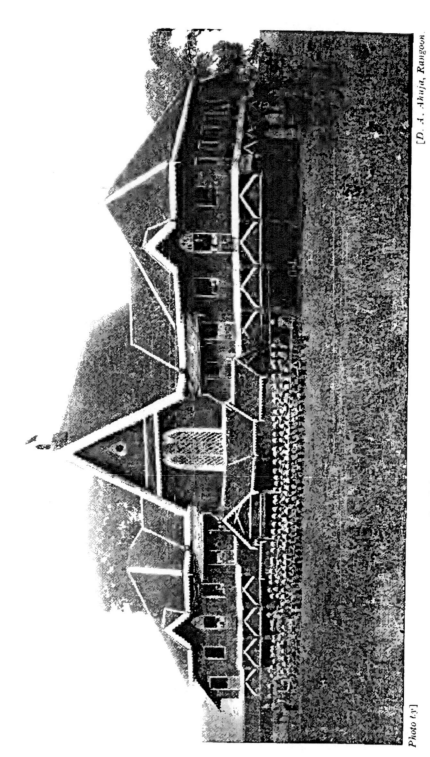

Photo by]

[D. A. Ahuja, Rangoon.

St. John's College, with the Cadet Corps.

[Facing p. 36.

INTRODUCTION

English education, and who realize the privileges and responsibilities they enjoy as citizens of the British Empire.

In this connection it may be of value to quote the Orders passed by the Government with regard to St. John's College Cadet Corps in 1885 :

" *The Cadet Company of St. John's College, Rangoon, has for several years past contained more than ten per cent. of Burmese lads, and this Company has at repeated inspections acquitted itself well under the circumstances. I am to say that St. John's College Company can retain its Burmese Cadets who are already efficient, even though they exceed ten per cent. of the whole Company. But for the future, no more Burmese Cadets should be enrolled until the proper proportion of non-European Cadets is brought down to ten per cent. of the Cadet Company. When once the proportion of such Cadets has been reduced to ten per cent., it must not be allowed to exceed that proportion in future.*"

Dr. Marks was for many years honorary chaplain of the Rangoon volunteers, and he was awarded the Volunteer Decoration for his long and devoted service. He was very proud of his decoration, and always wore the insignia pinned to his scarf when he conducted or assisted at divine service.

Of his other activities in public life, it is sufficient to remark that he was for many years an active and zealous Freemason.

CHAPTER I

THE OUTWARD JOURNEY

IT was a bleak winter afternoon in 1859 when I appeared before the committee of the Society for the Propagation of the Gospel at the office at 79, Pall Mall, and interviewed the Rev. Ernest Hawkins and the Rev. W. T. Bullock, the secretaries.

Few and short were the questions put to me, as I was very well known, and the catechism which was propounded went very much in these words :

" Where do you wish to go ? "

" Anywhere where the needs of the Society are greatest."

" What kind of work do you chiefly desire ? "

" Educational mainly."

" Will you go to Maulmein ? "

" With pleasure. Where is it ? "

" It's in Burma."

I did not like to confess my ignorance any
further, but taking leave of the Committee,
I went into Stanford's at Charing Cross, and
asked if they could tell me where Maulmein
was. The attendant in charge confessed ignorance, but when I said it was in Burma it was
known that it was somewhere in the neighbourhood of India, and so Maulmein was at
length discovered.

Of course there was a lot of preliminary
getting ready of outfit and other preparations
for a long voyage, for in those days junior
missionaries did not travel by the well-
appointed liners as they do now. My passage
was taken in the *Propontis*, Captain Barnes, a
Penzance brigantine of 235 tons register. The
ship was bound from London to Maulmein,
Burma, East Indies. The captain, two mates,
nine sailors, and one passenger, myself, made
her complement, fourteen all told.

I am not going to describe our voyage in
detail. Before I embarked, when I made
known my destination amongst my friends,
my report was received with consternation, and
several attempts were made to dissuade me.

I did not meet anyone who could give me any information from personal knowledge, but the country had a bad reputation.

" Don't go to Burma," said a Madras major, whose regiment had suffered there during the war, " you'll die of malaria in a month, and if you do not die of that, those bloodthirsty Burmans will kill you. Their great delight is to kill white people."

Another officer assured me that he had lately returned from Bombay, where he had had a bad attack of fever, and by all accounts Burma was worse than Bombay, and therefore he strongly advised me to choose some other country to go to.

I did not want for advice. It is astounding what an amount of that commodity of all kinds is lavished upon a youngster making his first voyage. Kind old ladies, of both sexes, with most philanthropic intentions, if they have nothing else to bestow, can afford to give advice for what it is worth. In after days one appreciates the motive but is amused at the recollection. But again and again during the voyage, I wished that I could have known what the voyage was likely to be. It was my first experience and I suffered accordingly. I found myself burdened with a lot of useless things and very deficient in things which would have tended greatly to my comfort.

The captain was a cheery, bright West-country seaman, very companionable and pleasant ; but the tedium of the voyage from December, 1859, to the middle of May, 1860, was more than I can describe. I had thought that I could learn something of the language on my way, and I bought all the books that I could think of. I had Judson's " Grammatical Notes," and what I was told was a Burmese New Testament. But it was Karen, and, of course, the two gave me no more help than did some Malay and Sanskrit books which I had also brought with me ! It was like trying to read Welsh with the help of an English grammar ! After several gallant and painful attempts to make something out of the mixture, I had to abandon my Oriental studies in despair.

I have often thought since, how well it would be if we had in London a bureau to give information to missionaries and others proceeding on their first voyage to the East. It would save them from many a foolish notion, many a useless expense, and enable them to proceed in comfort on their journey, free from anxiety and disappointment. They would know what to take and what they could get on arrival, what would be useful on the voyage and what would be superfluous.

It is amusing to the experienced, but painful to the inexperienced, to observe how frequently young travellers overload themselves with what they do not require, or could procure more cheaply, and better adapted to their requirements, on arrival at their destination.

The worst experience during the voyage was in the " Roaring Forties " round the Cape of Good Hope, where we encountered a series of storms and cross winds trying to the nerves of even seasoned salts, much more to a landsman like myself. We were tossed about most unmercifully, the only resting-place being in one's bunk, and even that was invaded by big seas that encroached on one's privacy and gave us more salt-water baths than we cared for.

But in later days I often called to remembrance how on the worst morning, when the storm was at its height, I opened my Prayer-Book as usual to read the daily office. It was the 22nd day of the month and the 107th Psalm : " They that go down to the sea in ships. . . . He maketh the storm to cease so that the waves thereof are still." It seemed to me a voice from Heaven, assuring me that, in spite of present peril, there was a kind Providence watching over us, in whose power was the sea and all that is in it, and that He would safely bring us to the Haven where we would be. And so it proved. We thanked God and took courage. The crew joined with me in praise to God who had preserved us so that we might pursue our voyage in comparative comfort.

To those of my readers who have had similar experiences in sailing vessels, in voyages of nearly half a year's duration in small cargo vessels ill adapted for carrying passengers, I need make no apology for this description of my adventure. But should any be tempted to follow my example, I would strongly and emphatically say : " Don't ! "

Still, it must be granted that the voyage had for me certain advantages. Mine had been a laborious and strenuous career, and a season of retirement for quiet reflection and devotion, with an ever-deepening sense of the importance and responsibility of the career upon which I was entering, and a sense of reliance upon our Heavenly Father's care, was of immense value, much more than I realized at the time.

CHAPTER II

WITH a feeling of the deepest thankfulness we came at length within sight of the Island of Kalagouk off the coast of Burma. I cannot say that my first impressions of the country coincided at all with what I had been led to expect from what had been told me.

Kalagouk seemed rocky, scrubby, uninteresting. I visited it afterwards in a Government launch with General Fraser, R.E., and we were in more peril going there and back in the well-appointed steam launch than we were in our sailing-tub!

I have learnt since that Kalagouk, like everything else, has its uses. It is being utilized, though under immense difficulties, by the Burmese Government for quarrying purposes. The stone extracted is carried over

46

to the mainland for the purpose of building
river walls to protect Rangoon from the erosion
of the river banks by the rapid current of the
river.

The beautiful range of mountains and hills
on the Tenasserim coast now came into view,
and soon the boat came to anchor off the
Burmese town of Amherst, where we had to
wait till the turn of the tide before proceeding
on the last stage of our journey up the estuary
of the Salween to Maulmein.

I went ashore for a few hours at Amherst.
It is a beautifully situated town at the mouth
of the Salween, which is one of the great rivers
of the Eastern Peninsula. I cannot describe
its beauties adequately. I have visited it
or passed it often since on my numerous
voyages along the coast, and never without
recalling that delightful first landing after
more than five months' confinement in a small
ship. I felt that if I was not in Paradise itself,
I must be somewhere in the neighbourhood. I
walked under a grove of cocoanut palms, glad
to be alone again for a short time. I confess
that I knelt down under a large tree and
poured out my soul in thankfulness to God

who had brought me safe to my destination, and I prayed that my coming to this beautiful country might be for the welfare of the people. The words came involuntarily to my lips: "The lines are fallen unto me in pleasant places."

My reveries were disturbed most agreeably by the arrival of some half-dozen Burman boys, merry, laughing, cheerful lads, dressed in pretty bright silk garments. In complexion they were only slightly brown, the hair, long and black, reaching half-way down the backs of some of them, and tied up in a bunch on the tops of the heads of others.

We looked at each other in amusement, not to say amazement. I had never seen Burmese boys before, and apparently they had never seen a raw missionary before. I certainly had no fear of them ; they showed no fear of me until I put out my hand and said : " How do you do, boys ? " Then they thought that I was going to hit them and ran away. I burst out laughing, and they, stopping, laughed too, and when I beckoned again, they came up to me, and we greatly amused one another by carrying on a conversation without a word being understood on either side.

I made signs to them that I had just landed from the ship which was visible coming up the river, and that I was thirsty; whereupon one of them, who had in his dress that wonderful *dah*—a marvellous bent knife, capable alike of sharpening a lead pencil or of hacking down a tree—climbed a tree with the agility of a monkey, and cut off two of the green cocoanuts; then, as rapidly descending, with his *dah* he cut off the top of one of them and handed to me the most delicious draught I had had for many a long day, cold and refreshing, more than I could drink.

This was my first introduction to the " bloodthirsty " Burman, and I thought then, as I have often done since, how incorrect is the sentiment expressed in dear Bishop Heber's hymn—written before he had ever been to India or Ceylon—

> " Where every prospect pleases
> And only man is vile "

As my narrative proceeds, I shall have much to say about the country as it was when I

first made its acquaintance. I will merely
remark here, in passing, that Amherst, before
the first Burmese war in 1825, was called
Kyaikkami, and that it was originally intended to be the capital of the newly-acquired
territory. It was named after Lord Amherst,
who was Viceroy at that time.

I had to re-embark on the *Propontis*, and
had my first taste of river navigation in
Burma, of which I was to enjoy so much in
after years. It was as happy as it was novel.
An English pilot came on board with his
native linesman and took charge of us, to the
great relief of the captain but not of the crew,
who had to be watchful and attentive to
Pilot Berry's orders.

As we went up the river new points of
interest opened out at every turn, while the
incessant calls of the leadsman, telling the
depth of the water, gave me my first dose of
sailor's Hindustani, that amalgam of East
and West, English and native talk, of which
I was to learn so much afterwards. I learnt
that *Bahm* meant " fathom," and that *Millani*
meant " No bottom reached." The river
Salween was in full flood and was a noble

stream, with many windings, pretty wooded banks and interesting villages. The houses seemed to nestle among the trees, to be built, the better class of wood, with thatched roofs of leaves (*Dani*), showing brown against the green. The greater number of the houses, however, were light and airy, built of bamboos, of whose multifarious uses I had yet much to learn. In Burma this gigantic grass furnishes poles for the houses, flooring for the rooms, thatch for the roof and vegetables for the curry, besides making itself useful in many other ways!

The houses are invariably one story, the ground-floor being utilized for cattle, buffaloes, fowls, and for cooking purposes. A very primitive ladder of bamboo reaches the upper chamber, which is the dwelling and sleeping place of the family.

Along the bank of the river we saw a specimen of " mixed bathing," and with most perfect decency and thorough enjoyment of the aquatic exercises. I did not, however, observe a single towel among all the bathers!

CHAPTER III

ON the afternoon of the third day after leaving Amherst we arrived at Maulmein. I had learnt that one may spell Maulmein pretty well as one wishes. All that is essential is to get the consonants right, after which you may put in any vowels you like. This is the case with the names of most of the towns of Burma. One frequently finds on the sign-boards of the railway stations that the name of the place is spelt differently on every one!

The name Maulmein is not Burmese at all, but Talaing, a reminder of the fact that until two centuries ago there was, in these parts, a Talaing kingdom and a Talaing King, quite independent of Burma. The Burmese conqueror Alompra, the founder of Rangoon,

52

Maulmein.

swept them away, and now the Talaings have almost ceased to exist as a separate people, and their language is all but extinct.

It was only a village when the British took it during the first Burmese war, but it became the capital of Tenasserim, one of the provinces which were annexed as a result of that war. It flourished wonderfully under British rule until the second Burmese war, when Rangoon became the capital of the whole of British Burma.

Maulmein and its Pagoda have been immortalized by Kipling. Its situation is most beautiful I have seen Burma from end to end, but I have never lost my first love for beautiful Maulmein. It is situated on the left bank of the river Salween, which is joined just above it by the large confluents, the Gyne and the Attaran. A long range of low hills forms the background These hills are covered with vegetation through which can be seen the houses of the English residents and the pagodas and the monasteries of the Burmese. Between the hills and the river lies the town proper, with its Government buildings, churches, schools, bazaars, shops and dwellings, and along the river bank are the wharves, rice mills and timber yards.

These last are a wonderful sight to new-comers. The huge and highly-trained elephants at work all day " a-piling teak " for shipment are a source of unfailing interest. With their tusks, trunks and feet they shift huge baulks of timber according to the will of the *mahout*, or driver, who sits on the animal's neck and directs its movements by means of an iron hook which he holds in his hands. Many curious stories are told of the phenomenal intelligence of these animals. Some of them are said to close one eye and squint down the logs as they lay them, to see if they are straight! Others are said to object to work on Sundays, and they all " down tools " as punctually as the British workman as soon as the luncheon-bell is heard!

I was told by my friends when I left England that I ought to provide myself with a revolver and rifle, " for self-protection " against the Burmese people, who were treacherous savages, and would murder any European on the slightest provocation. I declined this well-meant advice, and during my whole time in

Burma I have never possessed or used a fire-arm or weapon of any description I have never once had occasion for anything of the sort, though I have travelled all over Upper and Lower Burma. For five years in Mandalay I had no door to my house or guard at my gate. I have often been the only Englishman in large districts inhabited by many thousands of Burmans. I have slept in *Zayats*, or rest-houses, without walls, and with only my schoolboys around me, and all in perfect safety of person and property. I know that some people have not been so fortunate. But let every man speak as he finds. I have trusted my Burmese friends, and no people on earth could have repaid my confidence with greater hospitality and kindness.

From the wharf where I landed in Maulmein I went at once in a *gharri*, or cab, drawn by a Burman pony, to the S.P.G. Mission House at Moungan, where the Rev. A. Shears had begun a small school on lines which have been followed ever since in all our S.P.G. schools throughout the country. Children were admitted only on the distinct understanding that they were to be instructed in the Christian religion. No parents or pupils have ever raised any objection. But it would be wrong to suppose that their compliance indicates a strong desire for Christianity. Many parents wish their sons to learn our religion as part of our literature, but they express no desire to see them change and adopt it instead of Buddhism.

In the year 1869 I was at one of the stations on the Irrawaddy, where I wanted to start an S.P.G. school The people came forward very readily with money, and we had the offer of a good and suitable house, when all of a sudden the question of religion was mooted by one of the elders. He spoke very calmly and respectfully, and asked me if I meant to make all the pupils Christians. Before I could reply, another elder interposed, and asked whether the same secular subjects would be taught as were being imparted to the boys in Rangoon and Maulmein. I replied that certainly the same course of studies would be followed, adding, however, that while we would do our best in secular work, our great aim was by teaching our " holy religion " to make our pupils " wise unto salvation." The meeting liked my plain speaking, and after conversation among themselves, the second elder who had questioned me summed up thus : " We give our children rice as their daily food, and one or more kinds of curry, fish, vegetables or meat, as we can afford. All eat rice, so all must have secular instruction. The curry is like the religious teaching. We have given them Buddhism curry; this English priest brings Christianity. So both are set before our boys. Let them taste both and judge for themselves which they like best." This speech thoroughly pleased the assembled parents. The school was established and prospered in all things, until it was unfortunately burned down by carelessness in 1876.

Much work lay to our hands in Maulmein. Its extent and interest seemed to be bewildering. The first thing was, of course, to learn the language—Burmese. It surprised me to know that over forty different native languages were spoken in that Eastern peninsula. But though a knowledge of any of these would be useful, and a smattering of some almost essential, Burmese was the language to be learned, and a very difficult language it is. Unlike the languages of India, it is of the Mongolian family, and with slight exceptions monosyllabic. I set to work to learn it, not in the orthodox fashion with dictionaries and grammars, but by making my Burmese pupils my teachers. Whilst I taught them to speak, read and write English, they taught me to read, write and talk, and preach in Burmese. It was a very interesting process, and we could afford a hearty laugh over each other's blunders. But the result was highly satisfactory on both sides. We had no bitterness of learning, no sleepiness, but many an opportunity of knowing each other's mode of thought and peculiarities, and of forming a real and lasting friendship. My chief tutor-pupil was my companion for many years afterwards, and my fellow-worker. His son is occupying a responsible position as a Christian teacher in one of our Mission schools.

Then we needed for our school and chapel more and better accommodation. The house that we rented was large, but not large enough for our increasing numbers. So at last we resolved to make an entire alteration, which gave us a beautiful large hall with an *annexe* to use as a chapel, an extensive *tectum*, or covered play-room, and a swimming bath. Much of the expense of these improvements, and of the gymnasium which we erected, was defrayed by the liberality of Mr. Shears, who spared neither the time nor the labour to further the work of the Mission.

CHAPTER IV

SCHOOL WORK IN MAULMEIN

MR. SHEARS, the Chaplain of Maulmein, had arrived the previous year by P. and O. The house which he had taken was large and substantial, and, being entirely of wood, was easily capable of extension.

To begin a school in Burma is the easiest thing in the world. The Burmese have a natural love of being taught. It has come to them through many generations. As soon as a boy can toddle, he goes to the school at the Buddhist monastery, where he is safe under the care of the monks. If he wants food, there is plenty of it. His school equipment is of the simplest, consisting only of a black paper spelling-book, from which he learns to shout out his lessons at the top of his voice. Everything is of the most primitive kind, but admirably adapted to his needs in his infancy and early boyhood.

As he grows up, however, he wants something better, and the European who will take him in hand and continue his instruction at once commands his friendship.

Mr. Shears had gathered a nice lot of boys as day scholars and a few of them as boarders, and he had got together some Burmese assistants and a few Eurasians. This school-work at once awoke my interest. It was just what I had left home to devote myself to. It seemed to me that an excellent beginning had been made, but as I got to understand the language, and to look around me and see the possibilities of development, I began to feel restless and dissatisfied.

When I left England I understood that Mr. Shears wished to devote himself to direct missionary work, and to hand over the school to a person like myself who was experienced in school management. On my arrival, however, he did not seem inclined to hand over the management of the school to me, and as time went on, I became less and less willing to acquiesce in the manner in which it was being

carried on. So differences of opinion arose
between us which were not finally settled till
the arrival of Bishop Cotton, the Bishop of
Calcutta, in whose diocese Maulmein and the
whole of British Burma was then included.

One very serious question which presented
itself to me was the admission and inclusion of
the sons of Europeans into our Mission school.
It was to my mind unthinkable that we should
be giving the best education in our power to
native boys and exclude from our schools the
sons of our own co-religionists and countrymen

It was true that we were missionaries to the
heathen, but it was true also that we were
charged especially to do good to them " which
are of the household of Faith." A school for
European boys other than Roman Catholics
had long been needed, and a large sum of
money had been collected by the Chaplain
and sent to the S.P.G., with the request that
a trained competent schoolmaster should be
selected and sent out. But the selection had
not been made and much delay had taken
place, and the parents very earnestly begged
of us to receive their boys into our Mission
school.

SCHOOL WORK IN MAULMEIN

The Chaplain agreed that we would receive them pending the establishment of a separate school for Europeans, and the Commissioner of the Province, the Colonel commanding the regiment, the leading barrister and other residents sent their sons, paying, instead of the one rupee which the natives were charged, six rupees per month.

This added considerably to our funds and enabled us to pay our assistant teachers better and to improve our accommodation. Moreover, it interested the English community in our educational work, and made them understand the lines upon which we were working.

The practice of receiving European boys into schools originally intended only for natives is not, of course, free from danger. Not all such schools are fit for Europeans, nor are all teachers to be trusted to safeguard the admixture; but in the case of our Maulmein school it worked admirably and with perfect satisfaction to parents and pupils alike.

It required constant supervision and earnest care. The manners and customs of the different sets of pupils had to be taken into consideration and provided for. No preference could be shown either to Europeans, as the governing class, or to the natives, as being those for whom the school was primarily intended. But with care and tact all difficulties were surmounted, and the whole institution worked most harmoniously. To this day pupils of the several nationalities, who are now grandfathers, speak of their experience in our Maulmein Mission school in the very highest terms.

But the strain upon my own energies was very great, and that, together with the change of life and the privations of the voyage, told upon my health, and several times I was compelled to retire into a sick-chamber other than the single room in the school which was my home. All my illnesses in Burma have occurred at the beginning of the rains—*i.e.*, in May or June.

Never can I forget the exceeding kindness of everybody during those times of severe illness. The Civil Surgeon was unremitting in his attention, so was the Chaplain, so was everybody. The Burmese schoolboys showed their affection for their teacher by night and day attendance upon me.

SCHOOL WORK IN MAULMEIN

Let me give two instances of the kindness
which I received. The Deputy Commissioner,
Colonel Tickell, insisted upon removing me to
his house for quiet rest and medical treatment, and there the Civil Surgeon and the
Chaplain constantly visited me. An abscess
formed on my right side, requiring careful
treatment, and in those days we had no female
nurses, our only hospital attendants were from
the jail dispensary.

One afternoon in the crisis of my illness I
was alone in the Deputy Commissioner's house,
and a convict hospital servant was sent to
apply liniment. We were alone together, and
I noticed a sudden change in the man when he
saw how weak I was. He ceased to rub me
with the liniment, and with eyes glaring like
those of a tiger, he sprang at my throat and
tried to strangle me. I struggled with him as
far as my weakness would allow, but I felt
myself gradually sinking, when I made one
final effort to scream for help. The servants
came rushing in just in time to drag my
assailant from me. By this time he was a
raving maniac, and it was all they could do
to overpower him. He was a Thug, one of a

tribe of hereditary murderers, with whom strangulation was a fine art. He had been condemned to death for murder in India, but his sentence had been commuted into one of transportation for life.

The Roman Catholic Bishop, Dr. Paul Bigandet, a scholar of European fame, beloved and respected throughout Burma, had shown me much kindness and given me useful advice from the first, and he was a life-long friend and companion during our time together in all parts of Burma.

He visited me in my illness constantly, and one day he kindly said to me : " I know that your anxiety about your young school is retarding your recovery. I do not wonder at it, for I have suffered in the same way myself. But I want to try and help you. I have two Brothers of the Christian School who have just come from Europe, and who know English well. Let me send them up to your school. I promise you that they shall teach nothing that you do not wish. They shall merely direct the secular instruction and carry out your own plans and do just as you wish." It was a noble offer, but I could not accept it.

But I have never ceased to feel deeply grateful for such a generous proposal.

My love and admiration for this grand prelate deepened throughout the long intercourse with him in boats, in carts, in steamers and bungalows. " We took sweet counsel together," and often and often I wished that I could add : " and walked in the House of God as friends." That last privilege was denied us, but we often read together. His favourite author was Cornelius à Lapide, and we often laughed as I read aloud on board the steamer in my English pronunciation of Latin.

Let me tell one story of our intercourse. In after-times, when we were together at Mandalay, where he, like myself, was a *persona grata* with King Mindôn, we were one day together at the Palace. There was a large assembly of ministers of state, who were talking with the King on various matters social and political, when all of a sudden the King turned to us, and *à propos* of nothing, said : " What is the difference between you two teachers of religion ? "

It was a difficult question to answer to a Buddhist king in a heathen court. I turned to Dr. Bigandet and said: "Bishop, you tell him, please." "No," he said, "I'd rather you tell him." The King noticed our difficulty, and said: "You answer me, Bigandet." With wonderful French readiness the Bishop replied: "The English priest can get married but I cannot." The King laughed and said: "Is that all? And for that you want two churches to worship in!" But then turning to me the King inquired: "English priest, why have you not married?" "Because, your Majesty, no lady has asked me." At which answer there was general laughter, in which His Majesty heartily joined. "Then why not marry one of my daughters?" said the King. I had to confess that His Majesty did me too much honour, and I must remain single. What might have happened if I had been matrimonially ambitious I refrain from even contemplating!

But this is a digression.

It was a real pleasure when I got well to find the school buildings ready for a grand opening by the Commissioner, Major-General A. Fytche, in the presence of all the military

Kutho Daw.   The Buddhist Scriptures carved on stone slabs erected by King Mindón.

[*Facing p.* 68.

and civil officers, and of the merchants and other people of Maulmein. I think that it was one of the happiest days of my life. We had about three hundred boys of all nationalities— English, Eurasian, Armenian, Jews, Hindoos, Madrassis—while the majority were Burmese, Talaings, Chinese, Shans and Karens. All were in their best and gayest clothes, and the scene was highly picturesque. The Burman boy's dress is very beautiful. It is called a *putso*, and is about fifteen cubits long and two and a half wide. It is made of thick silk woven in wavy lines of various bright colours. It is wound round the body, kilt fashion, tucked in with a twist in front, and the portion which remains is gathered up and allowed to hang in folds from the waist, or thrown jauntily over the shoulder. The upper part of the body is covered with a tight-fitting silk or cotton jacket. Around the head a gay flowered silk handkerchief is worn as a turban. The boy's hair is jet black and very long, so that he can often sit upon it when he lets it down. But he oils and combs it very carefully, and gathers it into a top-knot (*yowng*) on the top of his head. We had at our opening a Christian

service and various speeches, and a short
examination of the pupils, and all went off
very happily.

Shortly after this, on Christmas morning,
1861, we were gratified by a visit to Maulmein of the Bishop of Calcutta, Dr. G. E. L.
Cotton, accompanied by Mrs. Cotton and the
Rev. F. R. Vallings, the Secretary of the
Calcutta S.P.G Committee. The Bishop wrote
afterwards : " A brighter inauguration of the
Christmas Festival I do not remember ever to
have experienced. Arrived off the main wharf
at 10.30 on Christmas morning, the captain
hurried us on shore, and himself ordered a
tikkagharri (hired cab) for us. At 10.50 we
were in the vestry of St. Matthew's, and at
11 I amazed the unconscious Maulmeinians
by appearing in full robes in church . . . On
Monday, December 30th, I breakfasted at the
S.P.G. Mission, and afterward began the grand
business of the day, viz., a public examination
and prize-giving at the Mission school, at which
I was to take the chair. Of the excellence of
the school and entire success of the public
exhibition there can be no doubt. . . . The
sight of the assembled boys, or rather the whole

examination scene, was of almost romantic interest. Nothing could exceed the picturesque variety of the bright colours of their *putsoes* and turbans, sometimes relieved by the dark dress of an English boy, and the blue jacket and trousers of a Chinese. They were examined for about two and a half hours in the Bible, geography, English and Burmese reading, and arithmetic, and answered remarkably well. They showed their English writing, and sang sundry hymns, chants, and even an anthem, with one or two rounds or catches, certainly with harsh voices, but in capital time and tune. The curriculum is certainly lower than in a good Bengal school, as may be expected, considering the recent origin of this. But all that is done is well and thoroughly done, and it is plain . . . that there is a large outlay on the part of the managers of zeal, ability and enthusiasm in behalf of the school."

The various reforms which I had introduced were approved and confirmed by Bishop Cotton, and all promised to be satisfactory, when Mr. Shears, who had suddenly changed his mode of life from extreme asceticism to married bliss, felt compelled to leave Burma never to return.

We all regretted this very sincerely, for though in matters of school management and other unimportant details Mr. Shears differed from the rest of us, we all had the highest respect for his zeal, earnestness and generosity in founding the Mission.

It was about this time that we introduced athletics on something resembling the English school plan amongst our boys. They had their own national game of *Chin-lôn*, a kind of football. The ball is made of wickerwork, strips of bamboo interwoven in bands, hollow and extremely light, and the game consists in keeping the ball as long as possible in the air without touching it with the hands; a circle of players, without shoes and with their loins girded, strike the ball in turns as it comes to them, with their knees, elbows, shoulders— anywhere except with their hands. To play it well requires much skill and practice.

Cricket was unknown amongst our boys until we one day had a visit from Captain Hedley Vicars (a cousin of the Crimean hero), of the 68th Durham Light Infantry. He was a famous cricketer and delighted in the game, and he gave our boys some lessons, in which they showed, as he said, " all the qualities that go to make good cricketers." He died a few months afterwards in Rangoon from the effects of a fall from his pony. But eleven years afterwards, being in Rugby for S.P.G., I was asked to call on his sisters, who read to me the letter he had written to them about our Maulmein boys' cricket, and they insisted upon sending a cricket-bat in his name to the champion cricketer of St. John's College. General Fytche, our Commissioner, most kindly made the school a present of a full set of bats, wickets, balls, etc., and good use they made of them.

From all that I have said with regard to the Burmese and Buddhism, it will be seen that missionaries of the Gospel have no light task before them. One thing, however, we have in our favour, Buddhism is thoroughly tolerant. Neither the laity nor the *Hpôngyis* (monks) have any objection to our teaching Christianity to old or young. *Hpôngyis* have very often brought me one of their best pupils, saying : " Here, teacher, please take this boy.

I have taught him all that I can ; now I give him to you." And when I repeat my formula that ours is a Christian school, and all pupils must learn our religion, they raise no objection. The one difficulty is the necessity we are under of requiring payment, for all the monastic schools are perfectly free, and *Hpôngyis* are not allowed to have any money. But we have generally found some means of getting over this difficulty. Some of our most satisfactory Christian pupils were originally brought to us in this fashion It was the case with the first of our new Rangoon school company that I had the pleasure to receive into the Christian Church by Holy Baptism. He was a pupil-teacher, a good honest lad. He went back to Maulmein and obtained the consent of his Buddhist parents. I baptized him by the name of Samuel in Burmese, in the presence of many friends of the Mission and of his school-fellows, in the Cantonment church, the service having been translated, though not yet printed, by Mr. Shears and myself. In the translation work I was very kindly helped by the Roman Catholic Bishop, Dr. Bigandet, and by several of the American Baptist missionaries.

CHAPTER V

ORDINATION AT CALCUTTA

IN spite of constant ill-health, I resumed work at the school, where we had enlarged the buildings, added a gymnasium, a bathing tank and separate class-rooms. Just at that time the news arrived that the master for the European school had been selected and was on his way to Maulmein In pursuance of our undertaking we had perforce to surrender our European scholars to him. The boys were most unwilling to go, and several of the parents declared that as they had not been parties to the contract they would not withdraw their boys.

One at least got up a petition to the Archbishop of Canterbury, protesting against this interference with the liberty of the subject. But it had to be done, though I confess that

I did it sorrowfully. The master arrived, a good schoolmaster for England, but incapable of accommodating himself to the ideas of the Chaplain and committee of the new school, and to make a long story short, the school was not a success and terminated in a dramatic disagreement.

Before that happened, however, my younger brother had arrived, and we had both left for a visit to Calcutta on the invitation of Bishop Cotton I spent my time in Calcutta as the guest of the learned and ascetic Dr. W. Kay of Lincoln College, Oxford, the friend and associate of Dr. Pusey, and his under-study as Professor of Hebrew at Oxford. I was also the guest of the genial F. R. Vallings, the secretary of the S.P.G., one of the kindest-hearted men whom it has ever been my good fortune to meet. My recreation was visiting La Martinière College for boys and girls, the Calcutta Free School and similar institutions.

In all these schools I took the liveliest interest. I felt that they were hardly up to the English standard, especially as regards the relationship between masters and pupils. There was a standoffishness which was irksome

to me, and which I felt to be not wholly bene-
ficial to either party. More mutual trust and
affection might well have been encouraged
without loss of dignity or infringement of
discipline.

The Director of Public Instruction, Mr.
Woodrow, was a man after my own heart, a
pupil of Dr. Arnold of Rugby, and a believer
in "Tom Brown's School Days," which I
confess to be my educational text-book. Let
me mention, in passing, that the then Bishop
of Calcutta was the "new master" of that
celebrated work. The Bishop lacked in one
thing only—geniality—but in everything else
he was excellent. When I sat with him in
Bishop's Palace and poured out my soul with
regard to Arnold's methods, he glowed with
enthusiasm, and once burst out, "I wish you
could have been with us at Rugby!" So
did I.

La Martinière College had a curious history.
It was one of three institutions founded by a
bequest of General Martine, a French adven-
turer, who made a fortune by manipulating
the jewels in the crowns and coronets of the
Princes of India. On his death he left a very

large sum of money for the foundation of three
schools which were to be named after him,
one in Calcutta, one in Lucknow, and one in
his native city of Lyons. He stipulated that
the education was to be given to European
and Eurasian children in the Christian religion.
The question as to what precisely was meant
by this term having come before the courts,
it was decided that a scheme should be drawn
up by Dr. Wilson, who was then Bishop of
Calcutta, the Roman Catholic Bishop, and
the senior Presbyterian chaplain! A very
curious document was produced and was
accepted, but the Pope, on hearing thereof,
at once prohibited it, and declared that he
would accept no scheme which was not wholly
Roman Catholic.

The management of La Martinière School at
Calcutta and Lucknow consequently passed
entirely into the hands of the Anglicans and
Presbyterians. The principal at that time
was a Cambridge Wrangler, a great mathe-
matician, a typical college don, a kind, good
fellow, but wanting in health and strength,
which prevented him from entering into the
games of the pupils. As director of studies he

was excellent. It was not his fault that he was not an Arnold or a Woodrow.

The Calcutta Free School had a different history. It was founded by Lord Clive with the spoils of his victory, and it has done immense good amongst the poorer class of the Eurasian population of Calcutta.

Amongst these children I found great delight, and I am by no means ashamed to confess that I made friendships among them which have continued till the present day. One of the most interesting memorials of my Ordination on November 1st, 1863—when the Cathedral of Calcutta was crowded by my young friends, pupils and teachers of the Calcutta schools— was a beautiful pocket Communion Service, with the inscription : " A token of affection, from the boys and girls of La Martinière, Calcutta," and a Bible inscribed : " Presented to the Rev. J. E. Marks by the pupil teachers and boys of the Calcutta Free School, as a small memento of their gratitude for the interest he took in their welfare, and of their affection for the kindness he showed towards them at all times, especially by promoting their amusements."

CHAPTER VI

BEGINNING WORK IN RANGOON

AFTER my Ordination, Bishop Cotton decided that I should go to Rangoon to start a new school there. In the meanwhile, I was to visit Akyab, to hold services there on my way to Rangoon.

At Akyab I was warmly received by the Commissioner, General Ardagh, and during the fortnight that I spent there as his guest I held daily services. Before my departure, a meeting was held under the chairmanship of the Commissioner, and substantial help was given to the new Mission. Some of the principal native officials and merchants begged me to take their sons with me to Rangoon, and I took eight or nine lads, who proved the most troublesome that I have ever had.

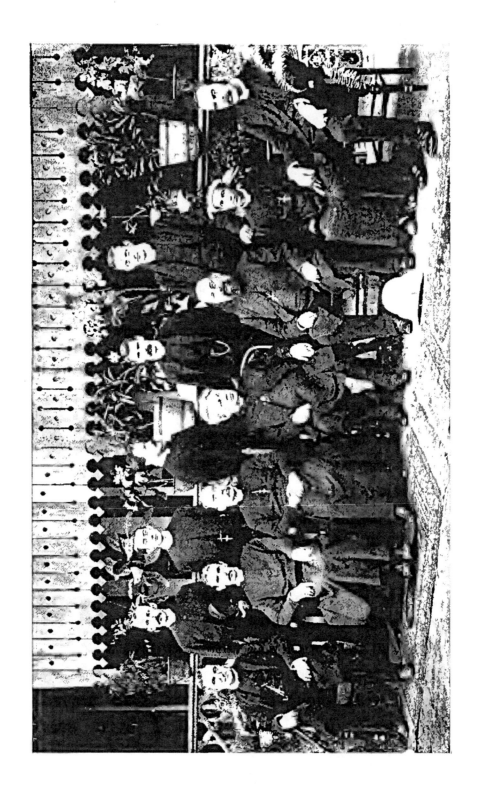

Several of them bolted back to Akyab, as they could not endure the separation from their parents and native country and the discipline of a boarding school. I liked Arakanese boys least of all my pupils. But yet one, the least promising of the runaways, afterwards became a trusted and titled officer of Government, and a most loyal, generous and efficient supporter of our Missions, himself being an earnest Christian and lay reader. One of our S.P.G. churches in Upper Burma owes its existence almost entirely to his liberality and exertions. I confess that I felt rebuked when, a few years ago, I baptized in his house at Poungdé three of his children. "Thou canst not tell whether shall prosper either this or that, or whether they both shall be alike good."

One other incident of my sojourn in Akyab must be mentioned. Some Chins, a hill tribe from the Arakan Yoma mountains, came into the town and sought me one morning. They were very scantily dressed, their hair was knotted over their forehead, and they had to speak by an interpreter. They said: "Several years ago some white teachers told us out of a book of the Great God who rules over all the universe and orders our lives. They promised to teach us more fully, and we are most anxious to learn. Can you come to our hills and teach us and our children ? We will take all care of you, and give you of our best." I was obliged to decline their invitation, but promised to do what I could to supply them with a teacher. But though I have frequently tried, I have never been able to send them one to instruct them. Yet they are our fellow-subjects, and have been so for more than seventy years. But the Church of England has never been able to do anything for them. Bishop Titcomb, indeed, wrote through Archbishop Tait to the American Church, begging their Bishops to take up the Missions to Arakan. But that Church felt itself unable to comply with this request. Must these hill-people always be neglected ?

On my arrival in Rangoon my old friends very cordially welcomed me, and gave me the most kind and valuable assistance with regard to the new Mission. Especially was this the case with that noble ruler, Sir Arthur Purvis Phayre, the first Chief Commissioner of British

Burma. Under him the three provinces had just been united, and the foundation laid of that prosperity which has ever since been characteristic of Burma.

He was a grand type of the British ruler. He loved the people whom he governed, and they reciprocated his affection. He was a good Christian man, the helper and supporter of every good work. To myself personally he was more than a friend, ever ready with his advice and means to assist in the Mission. The officiating Chaplain, the Rev. John Clough, also gave me substantial help, as did the permanent Chaplain, the real founder of the Mission, the Rev. H. W. Crofton, on his return from furlough. I preached to a very large congregation in Christ Church, Rangoon, on the first Sunday after my arrival. My text was, " Thy kingdom come," and I explained the necessity and promises of our Mission work. The church is a large iron structure It used to be said of it that, with a little alteration, it would make a capital goods-shed for a rail-way-station, and that if you closed the doors and windows you could bake bread in it during the middle of the day, in the hottest months.

But the efforts of successive chaplains have greatly improved its interior, and although essentially unsuitable, it has now a very ecclesiastical appearance inside.

On the following day we had a well-attended public meeting under the presidency of Sir A. Phayre, who with other speakers gave the Mission and myself a very hearty welcome. Then for the next few days I went round for subscriptions. If I have earned the title of a hardened beggar, the success which attended my first efforts must be pleaded as my excuse. I met with nothing but the greatest kindness and sympathy. Sir Arthur Phayre headed my subscription list with a donation of Rs 500, and Rs. 15 *per mensem*. Messrs. Gillanders, Arbuthnot & Co gave a like amount. In five days over Rs. 7,000 was collected, including Rs. 600 from the Burmans themselves.

I had to go to Maulmein to give over charge to the Rev. H. B. Nichols, from New Brunswick, who came full of hope and energy to continue the work. As soon as possible I returned to Rangoon with ten of my best pupils from Maulmein, to begin our new Mission school.

BEGINNING WORK IN RANGOON

My brother also came, as did a bright, good-looking Madrassi youth, named Kristnasawmy. His father was a commissioned officer of good standing and repute in the Madras Army. When the regiment was ordered to India, the boy begged earnestly to be allowed to stay with me. For some time the father refused, but at length, on my promise to look after the lad as my own son, and not to force or bribe him to change his religion, the Soubadhar left him in my care. He was most useful and efficient ; a better helper I never had. It was not for several years afterwards that he asked to be received into Christ's fold At his baptism by me in Holy Trinity pro-cathedral, Rangoon, of which I was then minister, the General commanding the province and many of the officers of the garrison attended to witness his reception into the Church. He was afterwards the valued Headmaster of St. Luke's Mission School, S.P.G., and was ordained deacon and priest in 1879 and 1881 by the Bishop of Rangoon. The Rev. John Kristna was an excellent linguist, and preached with acceptance to the British soldiers at Toungoo and Thayetmyo, and to the Christian Madrassis,

Telugoos, Burmese, and Karens in their own languages. He died in 1898.

We began our Rangoon school on March 14th, 1864, in a small house called " The Cottage," near our present premises. We paid Rs. 100 a month for it. I had one sitting-room and a combined bed and bath-room for myself; other masters had similar accommodation, and there was room for about twenty boarders, and two halls for day-scholars. It was the best house that we could then hire, but it was terribly inconvenient. The morning sun shone fiercely into my room, and made me feel ill and tired before the day's work was well begun.

The boarders soon got an idea that the house was haunted, and I felt it to be highly necessary that they should find out the cause for their alarm, or they would assuredly run away and injure our prospects. The lads complained that they were annoyed by sounds of rapping and knocking at the partition planks of their room. I promised to sit up all night and discover the cause, and the boys went to sleep. At dawn, feeling that as the night had been perfectly quiet no ghost would disturb the place that morning, I determined to snatch an hour's sleep, for I was very tired, and had a heavy day's work before me. I had scarcely thrown myself on my mat when I heard a shriek from the boys, followed by a stampede from their rooms into the compound, where they stood together, big and little, in real terror. The rapping had recommenced more violently than before. My assistants and I proceeded to investigate the cause, and it was not far to seek. My dear little dog had got through a broken pane into an *almirah*, or cupboard with glass doors, and to rid himself of the fleas, with which the floor was infested, was scratching himself and knocking the stump of his tail on the shelf. This shook the glass and the door, and thus produced the dreaded noises. The little dog, apparently to convince the boys, went through the performance in their presence, till they were heartily ashamed of themselves. But though they never liked me to refer to this incident, I always found them remarkably timid and unreasonable in such matters.

Older than the Buddhism, which is now the prevailing religion of the country, there was

(or I ought to say is) a superstitious worship
and dread of spirits, or *nats*, good and evil,
who are attached to trees, rivers, mountains
and valleys, and who work benefits or troubles
to people in the night and in solitariness. It
is a very bad and exaggerated form of English
children's notions of fairies and bogies.

CHAPTER VII

FIRST FURLOUGH IN ENGLAND

THE work of our new school was pro-
gressing very happily, but its very
success brought us trouble. The pupils admitted and seeking admission were too many,
the house was unsuitable, the work too much,
and I could not get my promised colleague.
We were cheered by a visit from the genial
and learned Archdeacon Pratt, who met the
Provisional Committee which I had formed
to manage the large sums of money entrusted
to me, and he gave us excellent advice as to
our future work, especially as to building new
and suitable premises. But a few days after
he had gone up-country on Visitation, when all
things in the Mission seemed to be so promising,
I was suddenly struck down with a dangerous
illness. A shivering fit came over me at mid-
day, my limbs refused their office, and I was

carried out by my boys to a kind friend's house
in the Cantonment, the part of the town where
the military live. The doctors who were summoned said that I was suffering from internal
abscess and that I must be sent to England
immediately.

It was a sad blow, but there was no appeal.
The Principal Medical Officer of the British
troops and the Civil Surgeon concurred with
the other doctors' verdict, only doubting if
I could reach England alive. So, leaving the
school in the care of the Chaplain and my
youthful brother, I was put on board the
British India steamer for Calcutta, thence to
proceed by the P. and O. vessel. My heart
was very sad, for I was very ill and troubled.
Four officers put me on board, and I distinctly
heard Colonel Phayre say to the others:
" Poor fellow! I'm afraid that that is the last
we shall see of him, and I did hope that he was
good for many years' work." (It is sad to
think that all the four kind officers are dead:
Colonel (afterwards General) Sir Arthur P.
Phayre, Captain (afterwards Colonel) Sir Edward B. Sladen, Captain Craig, R.A., and
Lieutenant Bagge, R.E.)

FIRST FURLOUGH IN ENGLAND

I must not omit to relate that the sad news of the death of the Rev. H. B. Nichols, who had succeeded me in Maulmein, reached us a day or two before I left Burma. He had dined with us and Archdeacon Pratt only a week or two previously on his return to Calcutta, when he seemed in perfect health. He was married in Calcutta, but on his way back he was seized with brain fever, of which he died just as he was landed in Maulmein.

In Calcutta I was treated with the greatest kindness by the Rev. F. R. Vallings and by Dr Francis, the Presidency Surgeon, who warned me of my danger and of the uncertainty of my reaching England. But by God's good hand upon me, the crisis was passed soon after we left the Hoogly, and on our arrival at the Point de Galle I was enabled to go ashore and with much help to visit the S.P.G. Mission at Buona Vista. The result of that visit was that my elder brother, the Rev. Philip Marks, and his devoted wife took charge of that Mission the following year, working at it with zeal and ability till their health gave way twenty-three years afterwards, when they accepted a less arduous post at Trincomali.

The officers and passengers were all very kind to me, and amongst the latter I made many friends.

Amongst others, I had the great pleasure of making the acquaintance of Dr. Druitt, the learned author of the " Surgeon's Vade Mecum," which has gone through many editions, and is still a text-book with the profession. He had been in attendance upon the late Lord Hobart, Governor of Madras, until his death. From Dr. Druitt I received valuable hints which have been of great service to me in regulating my life in the East.

Another of my fellow-passengers was Lieutenant George Hope Lloyd Verney, of the Rifle Brigade, who was exceedingly kind and useful to me, invalid as I was, and laid the foundation of a lasting friendship which has continued unbroken till the present day.

Another distinguished acquaintance that I made was that of M. de Lesseps, the celebrated engineer of the Suez Canal, then in course of completion. The kindness and assistance of these and other fellow-passengers made my voyage through the Mediterranean easy and comfortable, and my reception at home seemed to inspire me with such vigour and life that in the first few days of my return I wished immediately to go back to Burma.

But I was soon undeceived. A few minutes' walk told me of my weakness and of troubles which required careful medical treatment, so that I was compelled, sorely against my will, to rest awhile. Invitations came to me from friends whom I had known or who had known of my work in India and Burma, but I found that, go where I would, their cry was : " You must rest as much as possible, but *do* give us one or two sermons !" And this, not alone in village and town churches, but in St. Mary's, Oxford, and several cathedrals. Frequently, with every desire to please my kind hosts, I had scarcely strength to mount the pulpits or carry out other arrangements, and yet I felt that I was doing good service, not only for Missions in general, but for Burma in particular.

I visited for the first time St. Augustine's College, Canterbury, and deeply thankful have I been ever since for that visit and its results.

I was very weak from my illness and in agony with sciatica, and I must have presented a sorry figure as I lamely walked up the hall leaning on the arm of the Rev. Dr. Bailey, the Warden, past the ranks of the students, who regarded me with pity and curiosity.

In spite of my pain, I could not help laughing at the idea that I was like a wounded soldier trying to induce men to go to the seat of war. Nothing could exceed the kindness of the good Warden and his colleagues. In the evening I gave an address to the students in Hall. I stood by the big fire and felt much better. I am free to confess that I pleaded the cause of our Burma Mission with an earnestness that I had never experienced before.

I had prayed for help and guidance in this effort, and felt that my prayer was answered. The students were enthusiastic, and the Warden assured me that I should obtain recruits. The next day I had much private conversation with the students about Burma and India. As I was sitting in the Warden's room, a student came in to transact some business with him. When he left the Warden said : " That is Fairclough, and if you can get him you will get our best man."

He asked Mr. Fairclough to show me St. Martin's Church, and while there I begged him to come out with me. He confessed that he would greatly like to do so but for one objection, which I was able to remove. As we were going through the workshops the next day, the Warden pointed out a student who was stooping down to a piece of carpentering, and whispered : " That is Warren, a capital second year man." So I put my hand on his shoulder and said : " Warren, will you come to Burma ? " He answered at once with a smile : " Yes, certainly, when my time comes." The joy and thankfulness of that visit have never left me. The Church in Burma owes a deep debt of gratitude to St. Augustine's College, Canterbury. Many of its clergy and one of its bishops (the Right Rev. Bishop Strachan) have received their training there.

My friend the Rev. Dr Kay had left India and returned to Oxford, where he most kindly received me and most earnestly desired me to husband my health and to accumulate power

for future work in the Mission field. Again
and again I forgot the sage aphorism, "A
man can't do more than he can," and I did so
to my cost. The Society's physician was
Dr. George Budd, one of a noble band of
brothers, kind, considerate and sympathetic.
But he took a very gloomy view of my condition, which did not improve after repeated
visits to him. His patience at last seemed
on the point of exhaustion when he said to
me : " I willingly give my services free to your
Society, and if I thought that there was any
hope for your recovery, I would continue to
receive your visits ; but, as you perceive, my
time is valuable, and it is useless for me to hold
out any encouragement to you. Candidly, I
consider that you will never be fit to return to
Burma again."

It was a heavy blow, but I would not give
up hope. I asked him to afford me a final
interview at the end of a month. During that
interval I ascertained that he had what we
call in India a *shoke*, a bias, for filtration of
drinking water, and that he was especially
interested in a well-known filter.

I thought that I could work upon that and

Photo by] [D. A. Ahuja, Rangoon.

Mandalay. The Palace.

[Facing page 96.

I was not mistaken. At the appointed time I paid my visit, and said that I attributed much of my trouble to the bad unfiltered water that I had been drinking in Burma. " I notice that you have a peculiar filter, such as I should like to take with me on my return. I am sure that it would be of great benefit to me in Burma, and its introduction would be a boon to the other Europeans in the country."

He caught the bait and proceeded to give me a long description of the patent filter, telling me where I could procure it. He concluded by saying : " I see that you are determined to go back, and though I cannot give you a certificate to show that you are fit, I will not oppose your going on your own responsibility." That was all I wanted, and after thanking him heartily for his patient endurance of my persistence, with a glad and thankful heart, I went off to the S.P.G. office to convey the good news to my friends the secretaries.

I met the assistant secretary, who, rejoicing with me, said : " Did you notice a young man leaving as you entered ? " On my replying in the affirmative, he said : " That was the Hon. Charles Wood, who has been to offer his

services to the Society's home work. I told
him that at present we had no opening, but
would gratefully remember his kind offer."
He was afterwards Viscount Halifax, the well-
known President of the E.C.U.

The Society was at that time deeply tied up
in red tape, but let me say that though I have
felt and regretted this defect during my fifty-
five years' connection with it, I have never
experienced anything but extreme kindness,
courtesy and affection from its officials. Not
one unpleasant word has been addressed to me
during the whole of that time.

One other incident of my sojourn at home
must be related. With all his kindness to the
Mission and to myself, Colonel Phayre persistently refused to grant us a piece of land
whereon to erect schools and Mission premises
in Rangoon. The Baptists and Roman
Catholics as well as the Buddhists had obtained large grants either freely or at nominal
prices, but we could not get any. A similar
difficulty had occurred in Maulmein. The
local government refused, and the Government of India supported the objection, but
the Secretary of State for India in London

reversed their decision, and granted us twenty-five acres of freehold land.

With this precedent I appealed against Colonel Phayre's refusal to Sir John Lawrence, the Governor-General. But with all his well-known desire to help missionary work, His Excellency felt compelled also to refuse. Being in London, I resolved, with the Society's sanction, to appeal to the Hon. Charles Wood to do for us in Rangoon as he had done before in Maulmein. With Mr. Wigram, Q.C., one of the Standing Committee, I had a long and pleasant interview with the Secretary of State for India. Mr. Wood was very courteous and kind, but firm in his refusal. He said that we might have one acre free whereon to build a church, and as much more as the local govern-ment pleased at the upset price. This was a great concession, as the event has proved, and with this we had to be content.

The education of girls is all but neglected by the Burmese. But they had shown them-selves willing to entrust their girls to our care if we had the teachers to instruct them. My efforts to obtain such teachers in Rangoon had not been successful, and it appeared as if I must fail also in England. But shortly before I left, the Rev. Sir James E. Philipps, of War-minster, introduced to me a young lady who was well qualified and willing to go out to Burma and superintend an S.P.G. Girls' School in Rangoon. The Society gladly accepted her services. I also secured an assistant trained and certificated schoolmaster, Mr. R. Rawlings, to help me in Burma.

This, then, was the party: Miss Cooke for Rangoon, another lady for Singapore, Mr. John Fairclough, Mr R. Rawlings, and myself, who met for a dismissal service in January, 1866, in the Society's House in Pall Mall, the farewell address being given by the Bishop of Oxford, the Right Rev. S. Wilberforce. The others went before me by a sailing vessel, and I returned by the P. and O., no longer an invalid, though not very strong. I enjoyed the voyage greatly. We had daily service on board, attended at first by few, but as the voyage proceeded by almost all the passengers. At Galle I was able to tell the Cingalese Christians and other members of the Mission that my brother and sister were on their way to take over charge of the Mission and Church work in that station. Although I had kind letters of introduction to the Bishop and the Governor of Madras from their respective brothers, I was unable to land there, nor have I ever been able to visit that city, though I have passed it several times.

CHAPTER VIII

RETURN TO RANGOON

ON my arrival in Calcutta I found that Bishop Cotton was still up country on Visitation, so I went on to Rangoon for a few weeks, returning to meet him on his arrival at Calcutta.

On my return to Rangoon I found that the work had almost to be begun over again. My *locum tenens*, the Rev. C. A. Berry, had not lived in the Mission House, and the teachers and pupils were disheartened, and much of the Mission property had been lost. Mr. Fairclough and Miss Cooke and Mr. Rawlings arrived, and though at first we all had to rough it, we soon got things in order. We soon had our school full of boarders and day scholars, as many as we could receive. We used the veranda as a sort of chapel. For

the girls' school we rented a house in the
vicinity, and we soon saw how suitable a
person we had obtained in Miss Cooke. She
evidently loved her work and her pupils, and
they loved her, and she led them gently and
steadily to love their Saviour, and to be fit
for Holy Baptism.

The work, however, needed more vigour
than I possessed. Dr. Kay had constantly
advised me to lay up a large store of health
and strength. I had not been able to do so,
and more than once I doubted whether, after
all, I ought to have returned. I had very
serious attacks of depression, which is not
particularly pleasant for a schoolmaster.
But again the promise continually recurred:
"Lo! I am with you always," and it upheld
me even in the darkest hours.

Financial difficulties pressed heavily upon
me. Finance was ever my weak spot, and,
knowing this, I had very early accepted the
assistance of the agent of the only bank then
in Rangoon. I had previously followed the
almost universal practice of depending upon
one of the largest firms for pecuniary accommodation. But my bank friend most kindly

undertook the business and so greatly relieved me.

During my days of illness, however, before I went to England matters fell into much confusion. I could not remember what I had done with considerable sums of money. I knew that I had received them, but how I had disposed of them caused me the greatest anxiety and many wakeful nights. Meanwhile people were pressing for payment, and though the amount was not large, it was more than I could meet from my personal salary, which was very small. I was at my wit's end, and at last called the principal creditor, who most kindly undertook to accept one-half of my salary every month in payment of the debt.

The arrangement left me miserably poor and actually in want, and I felt that a few months of this trouble would inevitably bring me to the point of collapse. I am free to confess that I made this matter, not for the first and only time in my missionary life, the subject of earnest prayer, and I arose from my knees encouraged and heartened, to put the best face I could upon my worries before school assembled.

RETURN TO RANGOON

As I was dressing, in a moment the whole situation flashed upon my memory. I recollected that as each sum had come in, I had handed it over to the kind treasurer whom I had not met since my return. I at once called my *gharri*, and went off to see him The bank of which he had been manager had assured me that there were no funds standing in my name or in that of the Mission. But he had become manager of another bank, which he had started during my furlough, and to this new bank he had transferred all my moneys. It was a marvellous relief I did not tell him how much I had suffered in consequence. He continued for several years our kind and efficient treasurer and I had no such worry again.

The absolute necessity of finding better premises for the Mission school and my own and colleagues' residence was forced upon me. I felt that we were in the right quarter of Rangoon on high and open ground ; but house accommodation was very scarce.

Fortunately Woodlands, a large house, which had been the residence of several heads of departments, who, I need not say, were our local aristocracy, became vacant, and I was advised by several friends to secure it But no measure of the kind could be expected to be executed without criticism, and that where it might be least expected, amongst friends of the Mission, who were alarmed at my ambitious schemes.

I was told that I had swollen head and that my success had made me proud. But after full consideration with the Chief Commissioner, Major-General Albert Fytche, I determined to secure Woodlands, with its ample grounds, large rooms and ugly exterior. Instantly the success of the school was assured. Pupils from all parts of Burma crowded into the new premises, proud to find themselves in such excellent quarters. It was from this transaction that I may date the success of our Rangoon school.

Several of my old Burmese assistants came to my help, and I had, moreover, the valued co-operation of colleagues from St. Augustine's College, Canterbury, the Revs. Fairclough, Warren and Chard, all ordained at Calcutta for work in the Mission as my colleagues.

But with this staff I had a large accession of duties, congenial, but outside my missionary work. First of all, I must mention that at Bishop Cotton's order, I assumed the chaplaincy *pro tem.*, until his lordship's approaching visit to Burma, of the beautiful little Town Church of Holy Trinity on the river bank. It had been built under the auspices of the Rev. H. W Crofton, after the designs of Pugin, and was a gem in its way, and the people of Rangoon were very proud of it.

It could not be but that with the considerable duties which fell to the single Government Chaplain's lot in connection with the civil and military population, the missionary staff should give assistance at the Town Church and in the district.

But the employment of missionaries as Assistant Chaplains had been vetoed, both by the Indian and the Home Government, in the time of Bishop Wilson, and, therefore, additional clergy were appointed, who received a small monthly allowance in addition to the salary which they received from the missionary society which employed them. This scheme was at work in India, but had not as yet been introduced into Burma. But, in the great dearth of chaplains, Bishop Cotton directed me to undertake the charge, and gave me directions as to what to do and what to avoid, carefully safeguarding the prerogatives of the Government Chaplain.

But when this was known in Rangoon, our Chaplain felt it his duty to raise a storm of objections, and got up a petition signed by several leading townsmen complaining that whereas they had been promised a whole chaplain for the town, they were being put off with half a missionary! I intimated to the Bishop, that if his plan were not carried out, he must release me from further English services in Rangoon, as the extra stipend that I was to receive went to the maintenance of one of my colleagues.

His lordship wrote back a very conciliatory letter, saying that his plan was only temporary, until another Chaplain or A.C.S. man could be appointed, which he hoped would be shortly, after his next Visitation of Burma during the approaching cold weather This letter changed the whole aspect of things. The Chaplain recognized that without the co-operation of the missionary staff he could

Rangoon. Church of the Holy Trinity, the "Town Church." Since demolished.

not carry on the double duties of cantonment and town work in Rangoon, and he gladly fell in with the Bishop's plan and the petition was withdrawn.

I look upon my services at the Town Church as one of the happiest parts of my life. The services were of a type hitherto unknown in Burma. We had a surpliced choir of boys under excellent training, and of gentlemen of good musical ability who gave their services gratuitously, and of a very talented lady organist.

The proposal to put the choir into surplices was supposed to be our first Romeward tendency, and excited a letter of protest, which was to be presented to Bishop Cotton on his arrival. My friend Mr. Connell remarked, with regard to this protest, " that we need not wait till Cotton came down, as it was cheap enough in Rangoon already ! "

Alas ! Bishop Cotton's visit was never paid. He had always been deeply interested in Burma, and in his primary Charge he expressed his strong opinion that this Province ought to be separated from Calcutta, and that a Bishop with the gift of tongues should be appointed. He was to come to us for the consecration of the Town Church, when suddenly, on Saturday, October 13th, 1866, I received a telegram from Mr. Barton, of the C.M.S. in Calcutta : " Bishop Cotton drowned at Kooshtea. Body not found." He had been on Visitation in Assam, and on October 6th had been consecrating a cemetery, when, returning in the dark, accompanied only by a servant carrying a lantern and his robe bag, he was crossing to the river steamer by a single plank from a barge, when the servant heard a splash, looked round, and the Bishop had gone !

Though his two chaplains, Messrs. Hardy and Vallings, dived into the water immediately and searched about in the swift current, no trace of his body was ever found. Mrs. Cotton and their daughter were awaiting the Bishop's return for dinner on board the steamer. The news was telegraphed all over India, and the Government, in an appreciative note on his life, declared that it was the greatest blow which the Church in India had received.

I shall not easily forget the expression of deep sorrow and regret that prevailed in church

next morning when I announced to our large
congregation that the Bishop had met an
untimely end. I preached on Hebrews xiii.,
7 and 8. Bishop Cotton had improved during
his residence in India. His coldness and
schoolmaster attitude seemed to have given
way to affectionate earnestness and kindness.
Those who knew him best loved him most.

Dr. Robert Milman, a cousin of Lord Salisbury, was the new Bishop. He had been well
known previously as a Vicar of Lambourne
and Wantage, where he had done a great deal
to promote the welfare of the boys and young
men employed in the stables. He was, moreover, a learned scholar, especially in languages.
In manner he was a complete contrast to his
predecessors, Wilson and Cotton, as he was
most genial and witty.

He lost no time in visiting Burma, and in
May, 1867, accompanied by his sister, he
came to us in the height of the monsoon. They
encountered very bad weather, and were four
days instead of two from Akyab to Rangoon ;
but their welcome to Burma was very real and
hearty, and the time spent at the Mission was
very profitable to us all. Holy Trinity Church

was consecrated, Lieutenant H. R. Spearman acting as registrar.

I accompanied the Bishop in his special steamer up the Irrawaddy to Thayetmyo, our then frontier station, where he preached to the English garrison and performed a marriage. At every stopping-place—and the vessel only goes by daylight—he saw crowds of children, who appeared to be amphibious. He was greatly interested, and desired me to do my very utmost to establish branch Mission-schools at all the principal towns on that noble river. Miss Milman in her biography says : " From that time he began to feel a deep interest in the Burmese, ' the kindly and honest people who like the English and are liked by them.' " As soon as the Bishop had left us I began to think of carrying out his wishes. I could safely leave St. John's to the care of the Revs. J. Fairclough and C. Warren. Mr. Rawlings had been sent to strengthen the S.P.G. work at Maulmein under the Rev. R. Evans, and afterwards the Rev. J. Fairclough.

Henzada was the first place of importance on the Irrawaddy. It was the headquarters

of a district containing seventy-five thousand
Burmans. The Government steam vessels and
flats had just been sold to the Irrawaddy
Flotilla Company, which, from small beginnings, has prospered wonderfully. To our
Mission and to me personally the managers
have always been the kindest and most liberal
of friends. I can hardly speak too gratefully
of their unvarying and unwearied generosity
and goodness.

General Albert Fytche kindly gave me an
order to visit Henzada as Chaplain, and to stay
there ten days at Government cost. The Flotilla
allowed me to take a lot of my tame pupils,
and desks, forms, maps, books, etc., to begin a
school. We arrived off the town on a stormy
rainy night, and got wet through before reaching the Government Circuit House, where we
had to stay. The next day was Sunday, and
we had two services for the English-speaking
Christians, and collections for our new school.
All gave very liberally. The Burman magistrate offered every assistance, but I feared to
accept it lest I might appear to be compelling
the people to help.

On the Monday morning we went in

search of a house, and with great difficulty
found one, not a good or clean place, but
the only one available. My boys and I
worked at it in the pouring rain, washing it
thoroughly, and bridging the deep ditch that
separated it from the road, and which was full
of water. We were very wet, tired, and
hungry when at night-fall we returned to the
Circuit House, and I felt feverish and low-
spirited. But early next morning we got up
and went to begin school. We found many
intending pupils and their mothers in the road,
but the heavy rain in the night had swollen
the little river, our bridge was washed away,
and the water was up to our proposed schoolroom floor. Whilst waiting anxiously, and
thinking what we should do, my friend
Moung Kyaw Doon, the Extra Assistant Commissioner, came along, and at once solved
the problem by putting a very suitable house
(his own property) at our disposal, free of
rent, for half a year. In less than an hour we
had got our furniture arranged, and the
Christian boys joined us in a prayer in Burmese for God's blessing on the new undertaking.

RETURN TO RANGOON

We began school and worked very happily during the ten days of my stay. Subscriptions and donations came in liberally, a local treasurer was appointed, and the school prospered for many years. It was shortly afterwards removed to a new building, erected by local subscriptions and Government grants, and was then called St. Peter's S.P.G. School. Very many happy days have I spent in Henzada school. The best masters were Samuel Moung Ee, from Maulmein, James Simon, afterwards head-master of the Government Normal School, Maulmein, and James Charles. The Director of Public Instruction spoke of it as "the best second-class school in Burma."

Having been appointed Government Chaplain of the Irrawaddy Stations, on being relieved by the Rev. W. West of the care of the Rangoon Town Church, I was enabled to visit Henzada and other places on the river regularly and without cost to the Mission. Our best boys from St. Peter's were sent to complete their education at St. John's College, Rangoon, the Flotilla managers most kindly allowing all our pupils to travel at half fares. Sir Rivers Thompson, Sir Charles Aitchison and Sir Charles Bernard, successive Chief Commissioners, visited the school and reported most favourably concerning it. Bishop Titcomb, the first Bishop of Rangoon, spent much time at St. Peter's, and testified that it was "a first-rate S P.G. Mission School." After his resignation I ceased to be Chaplain of the Irrawaddy Stations, and became Chaplain of Tavoy and Mergui, and my official connection with St. Peter's was ended, and after twenty-three years of useful work the school was closed, and the buildings were sold in 1890.

I next went on to Myan-aung, then the headquarters of the district of that name. It is a long, scattered town, the Europeans' houses being built on the bank of the Irrawaddy, which is here broad and deep, and in flood time is continually encroaching on the town, in spite of the embankments which the Government at enormous cost erect and keep in repair. The people here gladly welcomed me. In a few days we had raised over a thousand rupees, enough to start our school in a wooden house which was lent to us in the Burmese quarter. A Burmese Christian master from St. John's was appointed, and he began well. In a short time the Education Department gave us another Rs. 1,000, and with the Rs. 2,000 we bought a large and excellent house for our school.

The people here were not so zealous for education as were those of Henzada, and I always had difficulties with the Myan-aung school, especially after the place ceased to be the headquarters of the district and many of the European officials removed elsewhere. After eleven years' existence the school was burned down through the carelessness of the master in charge. The Society's property there has recently been sold, and no effort has since been made to revive S.P.G. work in that station, though we have had many pupils at St. John's from the town and district.

I must tell about our school at Zalun, a township of 4,600 inhabitants, on the right bank of the Irrawaddy. The people were very anxious to have an S.P.G. school there, and the elders came to me to Henzada begging me to come to their township and promising every assistance. I went in a Burmese boat, for Zalun is down-stream. The

Burmans welcomed me gladly and hospitably, and for a fortnight I lived among them as their guest, eating only Burmese food in native fashion. Honestly I cannot say that I liked it or enjoyed it. It takes a long apprenticeship to discard with pleasure knife and fork and spoon and other accessories of European habits. But my hosts were all kindness, and did their very best to make me comfortable.

They turned the Buddhist *Hpôngyis* and their following out of a large monastery, or *kyoung*, on the Lamaing road, had it thoroughly cleaned and altered to my plans, and then gave it to me for an S.P.G. school. I had my master Moung Henry ready and we began work. For a time the school did well, but after I went to Mandalay and Mr. Warren went to Toungoo and our Mission work extended, the European labourers were so few that the school suffered from lack of adequate supervision. The town also suffered severely from flood and fire, and so the school languished and died.

The last and hardest of the river schools was Thayetmyo. This was a frontier military

station having half a European regiment, a
battery of artillery, besides Madras sepoys.
The natives lived in the southern half of the
town and consisted of a very large admixture
of people from Bengal and Madras, as well as
the Burmese. (In Burma, when we speak of
" natives " we always mean not Burmans
but natives of India.) But our missionary
efforts know of no distinction of race or nation.
The command is to " make disciples of every
creature." So the station Chaplain allowed
me to plead for our Mission in the garrison
church, and then the Burmese and others came
forward to help me to raise the thousand
rupees required to earn the Government grant
of an equal amount.

We began school in a temporary house, the
roof of which was made of thin tiles and there
was no ceiling. It was terrible work sitting
in that room in April, our hottest month—and
Thayetmyo is one of our hottest stations—
teaching about thirty pupils, mostly at first
Madrassis or Mussulmans. The school, St.
Andrew's S.P.G. Mission School, began under
difficulty, struggled on, and held its own. The
Rev. C. H. Chard, who became missionary and

chaplain of Thayetmyo, wisely and zealously fostered it, and under his able management it became a flourishing institution, as did also St. Helena's School for Girls, under the care of Mrs. Chard. The Rev. J. Kristna was afterwards in charge of Thayetmyo for a time. I must leave it to others to tell the more recent history of St. Andrew's Mission School.

That is the story of the beginnings of our river schools and of their subsequent development. It will be gathered from what I have said, and even more from what I have not said, that to maintain district Mission schools as evangelizing agencies, regular and constant supervision by the European missionary is absolutely essential. When that is not available the schools invariably fail to maintain either their Christian and missionary character, or their secular efficiency. But though the institutions themselves may cease to exist by the name by which they have been known and described, yet it must be remembered that no work for God undertaken in faith and obedience is ever allowed completely to fail. The results may not be at once apparent, but in His own good time, God will give the increase.

RETURN TO RANGOON

In Henzada our work seemed to fail and utterly to collapse when the school was sold. But on a subsequent visit to the station I was called upon by several of the elder ex-pupils of the school now in Government employ, who although only catechumens, yet held Christian meetings amongst themselves, and went out into the neighbouring villages to read the Bible to the Buddhists, and to tell the glad tidings of the Gospel of Christ. If we had but more missionaries to follow them up, many an ex-pupil would be found glad to hear again the lessons which he was taught in the Christian school.

CHAPTER IX

SCHOOL ROUTINE

BUT I must return to Rangoon. We soon found our new house, " Woodlands," to be almost as unsuitable for our purposes as had been " The Cottage " It was the residence of three or four European Mission Agents, of twenty-five Burmese boarders, and of 250 day scholars, whose schoolroom was very low and inconvenient. The house was costing us Rs. 1,200 a year and repairs. With the aid of our committee I had made several selections for a site for our Mission. The chief objection to all was their expensiveness—Rs. 1,000 per acre being asked for town lots.

I had at last bought provisionally six acres, when one day the Chief Commissioner told me that a most eligible site in a line with Government House was with that estate to be thrown out of Cantonment or military boundaries, and to be sold as suburban allotments at Rs. 200 per acre, and he advised me to apply for some of this in exchange for my other purchase. This I very gladly did, and after some unnecessary delay, secured our present most valuable estate at the upset price. I purchased it in the name of the Incorporated Society for the Propagation of the Gospel, which by its charters is a body corporate, capable of holding property, etc. One acre was freely granted by Government to the Society whereon to build a Mission church or chapel (a condition which has been too long delayed, but the obstacles to the fulfilment of which have, I trust, now disappeared). The land thus acquired as the property of the Society has continually increased in value, and is now worth not less than Rs. 10,000 per acre.

Meantime the name of the institution had been changed. We began it as simply the "S.P.G. Mission School." Then we called it "St. John's School," a title which some amusing adventures soon informed us was already appropriated by the Roman Catholic

Girls' School. So by the advice of Sir Arthur Phayre, and in accordance with Bishop Cotton's scheme, we called it " St. John's College, S.P.G.," a name by which it is known and loved by thousands of pupils and their friends.

Having secured the land, we now set to work to erect the building. We had offered a premium of Rs. 250 for the best design, and we chose that submitted by Mr. J. J. Jones, a young employé of the Public Works Department. It was by no means perfect, in fact it had curious and serious defects. But it proved to be a good plan to start with ; and though we have continually enlarged and added to our buildings, we have always preserved the main features of the original design.

The foundation-stone of the new building was laid by General Fytche, the Chief Commissioner, in 1869   The Rev. H. W. Crofton, the Government Chaplain, the Rev. C. Warren and I took part in the services, and all Rangoon, military and civil, European, Burmese and members of all nationalities were present on the occasion, which was one of great happiness to us all. I had very earnestly

longed for this achievement, and yet just as it was accomplished I was called away, and it seemed as though I should never be able to enjoy that for which I had so anxiously worked and waited.

But before I go on to tell about that, I will make a digression to speak about the fundamental principles upon which our schools were founded and developed They were essentially Mission schools of the Church of England, and from this we never swerved, either for fear of offending or from the hope of succeeding. On a boy's admission, his parents or guardians were distinctly informed : " This is a Christian school. If you put your boy here, he will be taught the Christian religion. No underhand method of fear or favour will be brought to bear upon him to make him change his religion, but he will be instructed openly and plainly in the doctrines of Christianity."

I can truly say that though I made this announcement to thousands of parents, never once did anyone object to placing his son in our school, and this was true not only of the indigenous races of Burma, Burmese, Talaings,

Shans, Karens, but also of Hindoos, Bengalees, Madrassis, and the other immigrants from India and the Far East.

Our religious teaching was the amalgam which held us together. Each day commenced with prayer and other religious exercises. The Christian boys, inclusive of Roman Catholics, Baptists, etc., stood out in front while we sang a short morning hymn, and I read a small portion of the Gospel in Burmese and English. We all said the Lord's Prayer, asking, of course, not for our daily bread—for that is not the food of the country—but for our daily rice! In our school we had but two meals a day, rice and curry in the morning, and curry and rice in the evening !

Very frequently I have heard the non-christians joining earnestly in our Lord's Prayer, and it gladdened my heart. After prayers the boys went away to their classes, and were there instructed by myself and my colleagues bilingually on the portion of Scripture which had been read, first questioning it into the pupils, and then questioning it out of them, until we were thoroughly assured that the pupils entirely appreciated the meaning of the passage From this practice we never varied. Even when the stress of secular examinations or Government inspections came along, we never lowered our flag. Some of our inspectors professed anti-christian opinions, and sneered at our religious teaching with these non-christian assistants, but all professed respect at our steadfast adherence to the principle of religious education.

After the religious exercises the secular work began, conducted on the lines of an English Public School. I need hardly say that no difference whatever was made in the forms or classes with regard to the various nationalities, creeds and languages of the pupils. The same rules and discipline applied to all. None ever claimed or received exemption.

The English and Eurasian boys received instruction in the vernacular, the Burmese learned English, and the interchange was mutually advantageous. We had to take the greatest care that the native teachers in giving secular instruction did not contradict our Christian or nineteenth-century teaching. Once I overheard one of our best assistant teachers telling his pupils : " The Burmese believe that the world is flat, but in this school you must always say that the world is round . . . etc." But though this English teaching was often very evidently against the grain, the teachers were most thoroughly loyal, and very honestly carried out the instructions that they had been given. And no pupils could have been more earnest, more keen, more diligent or anxious to improve, than were our pupils. It was the happiest school that one could wish for. The various nationalities vied with one another in their keen desire for excellence. They put in hard continuous work. I will not say that there were no exceptions We had some slackers and not a few disappointments. For instance, · a pupil would study most diligently and pass our private test examinations and give us every hope that he would be a credit to his teachers. But at the supreme moment—apparently without rhyme or reason—he would absent himself, to our great disappointment.

One particular case I remember. A student had done remarkably well in all preliminaries, and we believed that in the forthcoming Calcutta University examination he would take a high position ; but on the very day when he had to sign the roll for his identification he was absent and could not be found. When the examination was over, he returned to his place in school, smiling and happy, but he met with a very unfavourable reception, as may be imagined.

I demanded a private interview for an explanation of his conduct, and when he gave what I regarded as prevaricating replies, I thereupon administered exemplary chastisement. He turned to me, quite forgiving me, and said : " Please, Sayagyi, I got married. May I bring my wife to see you ? " My wrath was gone. A day or two afterwards the bride was introduced to me, a bright, happy girl, evidently a help-meet for him. I told her what had happened and that her husband had received the reward of merit. She smiled sweetly and said : " I am so glad, it will make him a good husband. And if he is not, I will bring him to you again." He came up at the next examination and passed triumphantly.

The Burmese, the Irish of the East, are like

our friends of the Emerald Isle, a mass of con-
tradictions. At one time, earnest, diligent
and energetic ; at another, lazy, careless and
casual. There are, of course, exceptions, but,
as a rule, they are affectionate, unselfish and
kind, but unreliable. I do trust and believe
that English Christian education will give them
that stability of character which nothing else
can impart, and I speak from experience

A favourite method for a naughty boy to
show his wrath used to be to run his head
against the wall and then lie on the floor and
scream. I recollect one Burmo-Chinese boy
performing that operation For a moment,
as he lay on the floor almost senseless, I was
frightened, but I hastened his return to consciousness and activity by the application of a
small bit of bamboo. It quickened his mental
and physical activity so effectively that he
never repeated the operation, but entered upon
a very honourable scholastic career, and he is
now a most learned savant and a member of
various learned societies.

The unreliability which I have shown to be
characteristic of the students with regard to
their studies was shown also in their games,

Lads could be keen, sometimes dangerously so, and then all of a sudden, apparently for no reason whatever, they would drop out of the lists and give way to lassitude.

I remember on one occasion an instance of this in connection with our Cadet Corps, of which we were very proud and with good reason. A company had been out to the rifle range at Insein, a few miles from Rangoon, for class firing. They returned in the early gloaming, travel-stained and weary, and the head boy came to me and said : " Sir, we are very tired ; may we have a game of football instead of evening study ? " I need not say that they were very lovable fellows. Everybody who had anything to do with them loved them.

Private study was the rule in the evenings, but no lamps—except the regulation *hurricane lamp*—were allowed in the dormitories. We had to take the utmost precautions against fire in our wooden buildings. It was a high crime and misdemeanour to infringe our regulations in this respect, and we were marvellously immune, though we had one or two narrow escapes.

When the industrious fit was on them, the boys would take their lesson books to bed and study as long as they could see, and resume in the early daylight. On one occasion a boy seemed to be unhappy and restless in bed, so I went and woke him, and inquired what was the matter. He looked wildly round him and then blurted out : " Pronouns have three cases, etc."

All the schools founded by me throughout the whole country were conducted upon the same plan, so that boys migrating from one to the other with proper certificates found themselves at home in their new school as much as in the one which they had left. These pupils not only in Rangoon, but in all the other schools, soon began a practice, which is continued to the present day, of calling themselves, *Saya Mat Kyoung tha* ("Dr. Marks' pupils ").

Naturally the education of Burmese girls was a consideration which weighed heavily on my mind, as it had on the cares and thoughts of many other educationalists in the country. We found the parents, though very keen for the education of the boys, careless about, if not actually opposed to, their girls being taught, especially by foreigners. The reply to all one's endeavours to interest fathers and mothers in the education of their girls was the blocking suggestion that it was not Burmese *tonzan* (custom).

We had to proceed warily. I was, and am, a celibate. None of the gentler sex were in any way connected with my work. Not one female was engaged in any capacity in St. John's College. I began, therefore, by utilizing the services of a Eurasian teacher in a hired room. It was a dismal failure. I then tried the experiment of getting a lady teacher from Calcutta. She was highly educated, and had a high idea of her own dignity and acquirements, and looked with scorn and contempt upon our primitive arrangements. Two or three girls were brought to her, but she seemed to think them young savages and to consider that it was beneath her dignity to instruct them.

About the fourth or fifth morning, when I visited the empty schoolroom, she suggested that she should take my photograph, to which I demurred, but she willingly concurred in my suggestion that she should return to Calcutta by the next steamer! So ended our first attempt, and we decided to postpone until my return from England any further experiment.

I felt keenly on the subject, and during my furlough I constantly pointed out how useless it was to continue the education of Burmese boys, if, on arriving at manhood, they only had ignorant, uninstructed girls to marry.

I have already pointed out how I succeeded in securing the aid of Miss Cooke. I shall ever be thankful for her connection with our work and its results. She had that magnetic influence, that sweet, winning way, that smiling countenance, which could not fail to influence the girls around her, and so St. Mary's School was started propitiously. It has thrived ever since, and is now one of the leading educational institutions in the country.

Miss Cooke continued in charge of the school until she married one of my colleagues, the Rev. C. H. Chard, who afterwards became Archdeacon of Rangoon.

Thus our educational work, both for boys and girls, increased and developed. Our greatest difficulty soon became the provision of assistant masters and teachers, but, as time went on, the schools themselves provided us with these and I have always found that my own pupils became my best assistants.

CHAPTER X

THE DIOCESAN ORPHANAGE

OWING to circumstances well known to all acquainted with Eastern countries under European government, there are large numbers of boys and girls of mixed parentage in Burma, most of them being the offspring of European fathers and Burmese mothers.

According to the manners and customs of the Burmese, no stigma whatever attaches to a Burmese maiden who goes through a form of matrimony with a European, though she knows that the union is dissolvable at pleasure, on terms considered fair to both parties. In the Burmese mind, the union between John Smith or Thomas Mc— and Ma Shwé, performed in presence of her parents and a select gathering of friends, the contracting parties eating rice and curry out of the same dish, is as much a valid marriage as if it were performed in church by a Bishop or Archdeacon.

This is the opinion of the Burmese. The Europeans set a different valuation upon the whole thing, which many of them regard as an amusing farce, knowing well that except by the constraint of their consciences they can at any time easily sunder the marriage tie, desert the so-called wife and her children, and depart to the home-land and marry an English wife.

They have not always, however, the opportunity for doing this. Fever, cholera, or accident intervenes, and the mother is left a widow with her children. Or the father is invalided home and the children of the Burmese liaison are left unprovided for.

These are our orphans. They are of European and Christian parentage, and cannot be allowed to grow up as Burmese Buddhists.

One can never forget the shock which one gets when this condition of things is first brought to one's notice. You go to what seems an ordinary Burmese house and the children come around you to talk. Oh, happy, charming creatures are little Burmese boys and girls! But as they play around, you suddenly discover the pale face and light hair of one which marks it out from the rest, and on inquiry you are told that it is the offspring of a former Assistant Commissioner or a young merchant, that there is no provision for it, and that it is being brought up as Burmese.

What is the missionary to do in the face of this kind of thing? We dare not leave the offspring of Christian parents to be brought up ignorant of, or hostile to, their own religion. On the other hand, we must be careful not to encourage parents to neglect their children by relieving them of parental responsibility.

After a very careful consideration of the whole question, I came to the conclusion that we must be prepared to take risks, and that the claims of these children, especially of the poorer ones, could not be overlooked.

Provision for the education of the richer classes of European and Eurasian children was already made by the chaplains under Bishop Cotton's Diocesan Scheme of Education. But for the poor and destitute and for orphans (with the exception of a small mixed school

in Maulmein) there was no provision made
by our Church in Burma.

It seemed to be a work rightly falling within
the sphere of missionary labour—at any rate,
at first. Many of these poor children were
being brought up as Buddhists or heathen.
Left to their Burmese mothers, they could not
speak English and were dressed either entirely
or for the most part as natives and very poorly
provided for. To rescue them and give them
Christian teaching and a good secular education
seemed to be a work of charity as well as of
necessity. And yet we could hardly provide
for it out of ordinary Mission funds

After much anxious consultation, I determined to begin within the walls of St. John's
College an institution called the "S.P.G.
Orphan Home," and I had mentioned this as
one of the objects for which I sought so much
land

We had wealthy fathers who provided everything for their children. We had equally interesting boys whose fathers were either
unknown, or suspect, or non-existent, for
whom no provision was made. They were
the veritable waifs and strays of Burma.

For such I neither dared nor would appeal
to the British public at home, and how to
maintain them on equal terms with the others
gave me many an anxious thought and sleep-
less night.

At last I resolved to call a meeting of all
whom I thought to be interested in the question. It seems that I blundered heavily. I
invited the attendance at a meeting to inau-
gurate an orphanage, of some who were too
deeply interested in the matter. It was a
large meeting held in the Custom-house. I
plaintively put before the meeting my difficulties and anxieties, but I got no sympathy.
On the contrary, I was assured that I was
attempting to condone immorality and to
promote concubinage. A proposition to commence a Church of England Orphanage was
almost unanimously negatived.

I shall never forget that afternoon. I was
utterly dejected, but my faith in the righteous-
ness of my cause did not fail me. I said in a
moment of bitterness : " Gentlemen, I thank
you for your attendance, I grieve at your
vote, but I am determined to establish a
diocesan orphanage."

THE DIOCESAN ORPHANAGE

Fortunately, we had strong support amongst
the clergy and other friends of the Mission.
One merchant, after hearing all the objections
at our first public meeting, quietly slipped into
my hands a cheque for Rs. 500 wherewith
to start the institution It has gone on doing
its beneficent work ever since—though after
the creation of the Diocese of Rangoon, at
Bishop Titcomb's advice, the name was
changed into its present title, " The Diocesan
Orphanage for Boys;" for on the establishment
by Bishop Strachan of the Bishop's Home for
Girls, the scope of our orphanage was limited
to boys.

The maintenance of the institution as a part
of, and yet to a large extent financially separate from, the College, has added very greatly
to our anxieties and responsibilities. For
many years I had to find about Rs. 1,000 *per
mensem* to feed, clothe and educate nearly
one hundred orphan and destitute European
and Eurasian lads. But it has been a work
which God has greatly blessed, and in looking
back upon my happy life in Burma there is
no part of the work for which I feel more
grateful, and which will, I believe, be pro-

ductive of better results. The Government
and people of Burma have supported it with
wonderful liberality and kindness. Let me
give one instance.

Sir Charles E. Bernard, the Chief Commissioner, the friend of every good work in the
province, promised me Rs. 10,000 if I could
raise an equal sum towards building a separate
orphanage in the College compound. But I
was taken ill and was unable to go about
among my friends to get the money. So
unwell was I that Sir Charles was good enough
to insist that I should leave the noise and
work of the College, and enjoy the luxury and
quiet of his residence, Government House.

One day he came to me and said : " My
promised grant of Rs. 10,000 can only hold
good for a few days longer, after which it will
pass from my control. I see that you are not
fit to collect your share. What could you do
with this sum by itself ? " I assured him
that we should be able to erect a building large
enough for our present purposes, and he thereupon passed orders on my application for the
sum of Rs. 10,000 to be given to us.

It was a splendid tonic. I bucked up, and

though I had already been having the attention of the kindest physician, this medicine
soon put me all right again.

Of course, as we expected, there came a
strong remonstrance from the Director of
Public Instruction about the grant. He had
cast longing eyes on this final balance of the
Educational Grant for the benefit of some of his
secular schools ; but Sir Charles soon convinced
him that the deed was done and that the
money had been paid into my account at the
bank ! Thus with a liberal grant from the
Rangoon Municipality (always our friends),
and a gift of Rs. 500 from dear Bishop Titcomb, who knew and loved our orphan boys and
was loved by them, we were able to build and
equip the very suitable Diocesan Orphanage,
which is the central house in our group of
buildings.

The Rangoon merchants have ever been
most kind and liberal. One firm has given us
for many years past Rs 1,000 per annum in
money or rice (we prefer the latter); another
has given us all the timber we have needed for
our constant additions and nearly every church
in the diocese gives us an annual offertory.

CHAPTER XI

MINDÔN MIN

AFTER the second Burmese war in 1852, when the Province of Pegu was annexed to the Indian Empire, a line was drawn across the country a few miles above Thayetmyo on the Irrawaddy, and Toungoo on the Sittang, all south of which was called British or Lower Burma, and all to the north (comprising about 200,000 square miles) was called the Kingdom of Burma, or Upper Burma.

By the terms of the treaty by which this settlement was concluded, it was arranged that the kingdoms should be separate and independent of one another, but that a British Agent should be entertained at the Burmese capital, then Amarapoora, and that there should be an envoy in Rangoon.

It was foreseen that difficulties would arise,

Photo by]   [D. A. Ahuja, Rangoon

but it was hoped that by mutual forbearance these might be overcome. Absconding traders would find a refuge in Upper Burma, where they would be safe from civil process, while political refugees from the North would find immunity in British territory.

Shortly after the conclusion of the war, or rather as the cause of its termination by a bloodless revolution, the foolish King Pagan Min was deposed, and his brother, Mindôn Min, was placed upon the throne The former was one of the worst, the latter decidedly the best, Burmese monarch of the house of Aloungpaya. Pagan Min, on his dethronement, instead of being murdered by his successor according to Burmese custom, was kept in honourable seclusion till his death from old age.

Of Mindôn Min I would speak with gratitude and respect. Personally, I found him to be a good Burmese scholar, a gentleman with much of kingly dignity but of very narrow ideas concerning the relations of his kingdom—or Empire, as he chose to call it—with other States.

He believed himself to be at least an equal of the most powerful monarch in the world.

He had a horror of bloodshed, and never tired of delivering himself of moral platitudes which did not always find expression in his dealings with others. I often thought, on personal intercourse with him, that with a little training he would have made an astute merchant after the Oriental type—" Heads I win, tails you lose."

He was of a kindly disposition, a lover of, and beloved by, children—a good sign in any man. He inaugurated a large harem. He had a strong sense of humour and could laugh heartily. He had a genuine desire for the prosperity of his country, of which, however, he knew very little except from the reports of his ministers.

He was a pious and learned Buddhist and spent large portions of the revenues of his country on the endowment of Buddhist institutions, while his military and other servants had to go without their pay.

In personal appearance he was every inch a King, though the nasty habit of chewing betel-nut and expectorating, detracted greatly from his personal dignity. He had a pleasant, low, musical voice.

MINDON MIN

The story of the founding of the new capital of Mandalay is well known ; but, for the sake of those who are not familiar with it, I will quote Mr. V C. Scott O'Connor's interesting book, " Mandalay and other Cities of Burma."

" In 1853 King Mindôn ascended the throne of Burma. In 1856 he grew very tired of his capital (Amarapoora), associated in his mind with the unfortunate reign of his elder brother and the humiliation of his country. He was anxious to make a better beginning, he was avid of fame, and he wished to draw away the attention of his people from the disaster which had overtaken his dynasty.

" He began accordingly to dream dreams, to see visions, and to consult with his wise men and his soothsayers about the founding of a new city . . . And so it came to pass that on Friday, the 13th of February, 1857— that year of terrible upheaval in India—the first stone of Mandalay was laid to please the King, and a hundred and fifty thousand people prepared to give up their homes and all their associations, and move to a new city at the caprice of his will . . . When the new palace was finished, the King and Queen went to it in royal procession and entered in. Here in the heart of his new city, and out of sight and sound of the British steamers which fretted his spirit, Mindôn Min lived and ruled for more than twenty years."

I have interpolated this long quotation as I shall have a good deal to say about Mandalay and Mindôn Min, and this statement of Mr. Scott O'Connor will enable the reader to gain a clearer insight into the conditions and environment to which the sequence of my narrative is now leading me.

Although Mindôn Min was the best, the most enlightened, and the most honourable King that ever reigned in Burma, his reign was by no means one of continued peace and prosperity. It was part of the compact by which he was helped to the throne that he should reign during his lifetime, but that his brother, the " War Prince," should be proclaimed " *Ain Shay Min,*" or heir-apparent, and that the War Prince's sons should be recognized as heirs-presumptive to the throne, to the exclusion of the sons of Mindôn Min.

ᶜ The War Prince was so called because of his official position as head of the army, and of his warlike propensities. It was his fixed determination to train the Burmese soldiers to be able to cope with British forces, and his constant endeavour was to gather great store of arms and ammunition in Mandalay. He employed many French, German and Italian workmen in his forts and arsenals, and sent the most promising Burmese youths to be trained in the military schools of France and Italy. His dream was to drive the British by force of arms out of Lower Burma.

King Mindôn, on the contrary, was of a mild and peaceful disposition He, too, longed for the restoration of the Lower Provinces to his kingdom, but he trusted for that restoration to the magnanimity and generosity of the British Government, when it should be seen how wisely and justly he ruled his own kingdom. He always believed that under stress of foreign or Continental complications Great Britain would be glad to withdraw her troops and hand back these provinces to him.

So strong was his belief that this would happen, that (as he frequently told me) he felt sure that he would eventually reign over a reunited Burma, and for that purpose he kept a number of officials in readiness to resume the government of the restored districts; though he always expressed his admiration of our rule in Lower Burma, and his wish to retain the services of some of our officers. Let me anticipate, by the following story, an illustration of the King's intense anxiety on this point.

One morning, when I was at the height of royal favour, a King's messenger came to me shortly after seven o'clock, saying: "His Majesty wishes to see you immediately."

I at once ordered my bullock carriage to be got ready, but before it could be prepared two other messengers came, each more urgent than the last, saying: "The King is in the Hall of Audience, and is impatiently calling for you."

I was at a loss to guess the cause of this unusual haste. But I went as quickly as possible, and found all waiting for me at the Palace, where I was ushered at once into the presence of the King, who, surrounded by his ministers and a large court, was eagerly awaiting my arrival.

Without any of the usual preliminaries, His Majesty asked me if I had had any letter from Rangoon, Calcutta, or England. I replied that by the mail which had arrived on the previous night I had letters from all these places. " Did they tell you the great news ? " he asked. I replied that my letters contained no important information whatever.

The King seemed astonished, and repeated his question in other forms. I could not make out what he meant, and assured him that my answer was quite accurate. So, still thinking that I was keeping back important news, he ordered a herald to read out loud, for the information of myself and others, a Burmese translation of a pamphlet of the " Battle of Dorking " series, entitled, " How the Russians took India."

I listened with interest and amusement, the King, with his binoculars, watching my face the whole time When the reading was finished, His Majesty, with great satisfaction, said to me, " There, English Priest, what do you say to that ? "

I told him that I had some weeks previously read that pamphlet, which was not history, but only a parable to warn England what might possibly happen unless due precautions were taken.

The King was incredulous, and said that he knew that English people never confessed to having been defeated. I told him to ask his French and Italian dependents, who, to gain his favour, had given him the pamphlet, whether what I had said of it was not true.

They, of course, were obliged to say that I was right. "Then," said the King, "I have been deceived and made a fool of;" and he hastily rose up and quitted the hall in great anger. People who had petitions to present to him that day were very unfortunate !

I have made this long digression in order that my readers may have some idea of the state of things in the Kingdom of Burma when, in the Providence of God, I was called upon to begin our Church's Mission in that country.

CHAPTER XII

THE CALL TO MANDALAY

OFTEN and often when my charge of district schools embraced Thayetmyo, I looked longingly across the frontier, and prayed that the way might be opened for me to extend my missionary efforts into the territory of the Burmese King. But there was either a clause in the treaty or a distinct understanding, that foreign missionaries were not to pass the frontier, and so, whenever I hinted my desire to go into the forbidden land, I was always told that the British Government would not sanction, any more than the Burmese Government allow, such an experiment.

But that did not remove my earnest desire, which I had entertained ever since I read on my long voyage Mrs. Macleod Wyllie's most interesting book called " The Gospel in Burma,"

153

describing the work and the perils of Dr. Adoniram Judson, the great American missionary to the King and Court of Burma in 1823–25.

I longed, under the altered circumstances, to visit and try to influence the King. Shortly after the amalgamation of the three provinces into the one Government of British Burma, Sir Arthur P. Phayre, as Agent to the Viceroy and Governor-General, went on a second mission to the King at Amarapoora, in order to negotiate a commercial treaty between the two countries. In this he was unfortunately not successful, and his failure was a profound disappointment. But from him and from Bishop Bigandet, who accompanied him, I heard very full details of the etiquette and customs of the Burmese Court, which they both described as the most ceremonious and exclusive of any they had ever heard of. And yet both were full of praise of the excellent personal qualities and disposition of King Mindôn.

But when I hinted to Sir Arthur that I should like to visit His Majesty for missionary purposes, he became very grave. He said :

"We have had two very expensive Burmese
wars, costing enormous sums and many valuable lives. Our relations with this King,
though he will not sign a treaty, are more
amicable and advantageous than we have
ever before had with any of his predecessors.
We have left him Upper Burma, which is most
useful as a friendly buffer State between our
territory and China and Siam. The King is
a learned man in his way, and prides himself
on being entitled the ' Great Chief of Righteous-
ness, and the Defender of the Buddhist Faith.'
He is a very devout Buddhist, and spends a
great portion of the revenues of his country
in building pagodas and monasteries, and in
feeding an immense number of *Hpôngyis*. The
Government of India is very anxious to continue on good terms with him, to the advantage
of both countries He would resent our per-
mitting an English missionary to go into his
country. It would be certain to cause unpleasantness, which it is our earnest wish to
avoid. You would most likely get into
trouble. We should be compelled to interfere
on your behalf, and then complications would
arise, and evil rather than good would be the

result. So I can neither sanction nor recommend your attempting to go to the King's country."

This from so good a Christian ruler, and such a munificent friend to missions as was Sir Arthur Phayre, was very disappointing. So I had to wait. But not for very long. One of the King's sons, the Thōnzai Prince, owing to one of those family troubles to which I have referred, came to Rangoon, where he was received with much respect and affection by the Burmans, who supplied all his wants and showed him all the sights of our capital. Amongst other places that he visited was St. John's College, S.P.G., then in its vigorous childhood. He professed great interest in a school where Burmese boys were so loved and cared for and were so affectionate to a foreign *Hpôngyi*. I showed him the boys' work, and he heard them converse with me in English. He accepted a Burmese New Testament and other Christian books.

He returned to Mandalay with Sir Arthur Phayre, and was shortly afterwards reconciled to the King his father, to whom he told of all the wonders of Rangoon, not excepting our

Mandalay.   The State Barge.

[Facing p. 156.

THE CALL TO MANDALAY

S.P.G. school. Months rolled by, Sir Arthur Phayre left and was succeeded as Chief Commissioner by General Albert Fytche, who had been a most kind supporter of our work in Maulmein. One of his first duties was to go to Mandalay to obtain the commercial treaty. This, owing to the firm attitude of the Government of India and his own tact, and the assistance of Major (afterwards General Sir Edward B.) Sladen, the British Resident, he succeeded. in completing.

A few weeks after General Fytche's return to Rangoon, I had the pleasure of welcoming to Burma from St. Augustine's, Canterbury, Mr. C. H. Chard (afterwards Archdeacon of Rangoon) to join our Mission, which was thus providentially strengthened. One evening, just as we had finished our day's school work, I received by special messenger a letter from Mr. J. S. Manook, an Armenian—the King's *Kalawun*, or Minister for Foreigners.

The letter consisted of a large scroll of Burmese black paper (*parabike*) folded in native fashion, with the royal insignia of the Peacock, and with the words: " From the King of Burma," inscribed on it in beautiful characters.

It was written in French chalk, but was evidently authentic.

It set forth that His Majesty, with all his titles, had heard of the school of the English priest in British Burma, and the good that the school had done amongst the people, and desired (commanded) that I should go up to the new capital city of Mandalay, the centre of the world, and there, under His Majesty's patronage and support, establish a similar Christian school for the benefit of his people.

Let me say here parenthetically a word about the *parabike*. It is macerated bamboo, folded in squares, dyed black, and the writing thereon is almost, if not quite, as permanent as that written on ordinary writing paper with pen and ink.

Promising the messenger an early reply, and making an appointment for our next interview, I went off at once with this document to our Chief Commissioner. When he saw the letter, General Fytche showed more interest and pleasure in it than I had ever seen him exhibit before. In India he was nicknamed the *Tanda Machla*, or the Cool Fish, because he was never excited. Opening his own budget from Mandalay, he found a letter from Major Sladen, telling him that the King had written to me, and was very anxious that I should accept his invitation. General Fytche was willing, but the consent of the Bishop of Calcutta and the Government of India was needed.

I felt certain about Bishop Milman, but anxious with regard to the Foreign Office and the Viceroy. But all was made smooth. I was duly told that under certain conditions I might go to Mandalay at Government expense as Chaplain to the English residents, and stay there a fortnight or so. Accordingly, on August 20th, 1868, I set out by steamer, accompanied by six of my best boys from St. John's College. At Thayetmyo, our frontier station, I received a telegram from Government telling me not to enter Burmese territory till I should hear from Major Sladen of his return to Mandalay from his expedition to the Shan States. So, both as missionary and chaplain, I went up and down the Irrawaddy calling at all our Mission stations, and wherever there were Europeans to be ministered unto. My boys were with me, and in order to keep up their

English they had to write a diary of each day's occurrences. But this frequently became monotonous. There is not much to be recorded on a river or jungle trip. This is a typical entry : " Your big. dog, Lion, stole your dinner and got a beating. We were very sorry for the dog, but very glad to have some circumstance to write about."

With the necessary information we left Thayetmyo in a crowded and dilapidated steamer on October 1st, and entered the King's territory the same evening. We landed at Minhla, the first station in Upper Burma, and went to pay our respects to the *Wun*, or Governor, who by royal order received us most courteously. My boys, however, came back wiser and sadder. According to Burmese custom they had left their shoes on the lowest step of the great man's house, and equally according to Burmese custom the shoes were stolen before the interview was ended.

The difference between the country under Burman and British rule was very marked. Physically the features were the same ; but the dwellings of the people in the towns and villages of the King's dominions were mean and poor compared with the substantial teak and brick houses of the inhabitants of Lower Burma.

We stayed one night at Ye-nan-kyoung, *the creek of stinking water* (*i.e.*, petroleum), where the petroleum wells were situated on a hill about one or two miles from the bank. With much difficulty I managed to get on to a bullock cart and ascend the hill and view the operation of extracting the oil.

I looked down a deep well, over which was a cross-beam with a wheel and a long rope attached to it. At the end of the rope was a metal bucket which was let down to a great depth. At the bottom of the well one could hear a bubbling, and a fetid gas exuded from it. The other end of the rope was bound round the body of a stalwart Burman, who ran down the hill and so pulled the bucket full of crude oil up the well. The oil thus obtained was emptied by hand into a bamboo tube, whence it floated down to the boats on the river bank. The waste through leakage marked the progress of the oil all the way down to the river.

The oil itself was like greasy treacle of a greenish colour, and was highly valued by the Burmese as a cure for skin diseases. The workers all enjoyed marvellous health.

This was the beginning of what has since become a staple industry of Burma. It was then, like everything else in Upper Burma, a royal monopoly, and the unfortunate minister or favourite of the Crown who received the promise of a boat-load of earth-oil at the King's valuation by no means congratulated himself on his good fortune.

First he had to get the oil, then to bring it to Mandalay, then to find a market for it, then to pay the various dues and duties demanded, and then to pocket what remained. Oh, the groans that I have heard concerning the transaction! The King thought that he was conferring a royal favour, but the unfortunate recipient knew better.

The wonderful change that has come over the production and refinement of this oil under British government is best illustrated by the balance-sheets of the various companies now associated with this trade which show that even in war time the profits of one of them amounted to almost £150,000.

CHAPTER XIII

FIRST INTERVIEWS WITH KING MINDÔN*

WE arrived at Mandalay on October 8th, 1868, and were most kindly received by my old friend of Maulmein and Rangoon, Major Sladen, the British Resident, who had much to tell of his recent expedition, and of the manners and customs of the Burmese Court. The *Kalawun* and other officials from the Palace came several times to see us, and to inquire on behalf of the King whether we had all that we needed. Mandalay was then a very curious place. It was surrounded by a low embattled wall each side of which was a mile and one-eighth long: it stood four-square, with bastions and imposing-looking gates, and very elegant turrets at intervals. A deep moat surrounded the city. Only the

* *cf.* Letter 1.

Palace, courts of ministers and law, and residences of the nobility and their relatives, occupied the enclosed space. The roads were good, wide, and at right angles through the city. Outside the walls lived the artisans and foreigners, Chinese, natives of India, Europeans of all nations, Armenians, etc., in all comprising perhaps 125,000. I held services in the court-house of the Residency for the Europeans.

On the Monday after our arrival, we had by appointment our first and informal or semi-state interview with the King. My boys and I went to the Palace in bullock carts, the most uncomfortable of conveyances. We had to climb in over the bullocks' tails, and the bamboo flooring sloped at a fearful angle. The wheels, consisting of one or two solid blocks, had probably been made round originally, but they had worked nearly square. The roads outside the city walls were terribly bad, so that by the time we arrived at the Palace gates we felt that our limbs wanted readjusting. We had to walk across the Palace compound, no umbrellas or sticks of any kind being allowed—only as a *Hpôngyi* it was permitted

for one of my boys to hold a large fan over
my head, or I should certainly have had a
sunstroke. We went first to see the famous
White Elephant, who occupied a large grandly
painted house adjoining the Palace. He was
a huge, restless, savage brute, highly pam-
pered and fed, but never worked. He was
white only in a technical sense—to an ordinary
observer he appeared to be of the same colour
as other elephants. He had killed his keeper
a few days before, and only acknowledged my
visit by throwing a bundle of hay at me.

We then ascended the grand steps of the
Hman-nan-daw (the true, or, perhaps, the glass
palace), having, of course, left our shoes this
time under safe custody at the bottom of the
steps. We found ourselves in a very grand,
large hall, splendidly decorated, with magnificent pillars of teak covered with vermilion
and gold, with large mirrors from France
against the highly-adorned walls, and the floors
covered with beautiful and costly carpets.

I entered into conversation with many of
the King's ministers of State, who were attended by their secretaries and clerks, carrying
their portfolios of black paper or *parabike*.

The ministers wore long, flowing cloaks or surplices of white muslin over their ordinary dress, and all Burmans had a small fillet of muslin round their heads. No turban or folded dress which might possibly conceal a lethal weapon was allowed in the Palace. Whilst thus talking freely, suddenly there was a whisper, " *Twet daw mu thi*," " the King is coming out ! " Instantly all took their places on knees and elbows on the floor, ranging themselves in rows according to their rank. I was shown my place, a nicely-carpeted corner in front of the throne to the King's left. Every head (except mine) of that large assembly was bowed to the floor. I had been told to sit, but by no means to let my feet be visible. It was an unusual and very cramped position.

Doors opened, one behind another, and far in the distance I could see one individual stalking onward in solitary dignity. It was the King, a fine, tall, typical Burman-looking man, about fifty-five years of age, very dignified but very pleasant, " every inch a king." He walked on to the dais, which was covered with crimson cloth, and threw himself down on a beautiful couch. Several of the princes,

Photo by]   [D. A. Ahuja, Rangoon.

King Thibaw's Throne.

[Facing p. 166.

all grandly dressed, came in at a lower door
and took their places near me. One of them
crawled up on hands and knees and placed
the emblems of royalty, the golden-handled
sword, the gold betel-box, and the gold spittoon,
before the King. His Majesty once, as a token
of his goodwill, sent a gold spittoon as a present
to Queen Victoria, who, in acknowledging the
gift, thanked the King for the beautiful flower
vase that he had so kindly sent her!

The King took up a pair of binocular glasses
and had a good stare round the Court. When
his eyes rested upon me, and my boys, who
all wore their school badge of S.P.G. on their
arm, a herald sang out in a kind of monotone
declaration a statement about us, that in
obedience to the royal command we had come
from Rangoon, and now placed our heads
under the Golden Foot and waited His
Majesty's further commands. Like all such
recitations, it ended with the long-drawn-out
U tin bah thi, P a y a, " My lord, etc."

In a very soft and agreeable voice the King
began to ask whether I had had a pleasant
journey to his capital, whether I was happy
and comfortable in the Residency, how old

I was, etc., etc. He then told me how pleased he was that I had come at his invitation, and he desired to know what requests I had to make to him, assuring me that all were granted before they were asked. I told him that my requests were: 1. Permission to labour as a Christian missionary in his capital and country. 2. To build a church in Mandalay for worship according to the Use of the Church of England. 3. To get a piece of land for an English cemetery; and 4. To build, with His Majesty's help, a Christian school for Burmese boys. With regard to the first, the King said that I had his full sanction to preach my religion in his dominions, and that no one should be molested for listening or even for becoming Christian.

I could not but remember what different treatment had been accorded to Dr. Judson by the then King, who spurned the offer of a Bible, treated the missionary with contumely and insult, imprisoned and tried to starve him at Aung-pinlai, and even purposed to have him devoured in a lion's cage; from which fate the missionary was saved only by the providential approach of the British army, when

his services were required as an interpreter.
Nor could I forget that only a few months
previously several Burmans had been crucified
by royal order for preaching Buddhist heresy,
real or imagined, and that the British Political
Agent had, by command of the Viceroy,
expressed the abhorrence of Her Majesty's
Government of such cruelty and persecution
for conscience sake. With regard to the
cemetery, the King directed me to consult
Major Sladen, and his ministers would give
effect to our wishes. We, of course, chose the
site next the Roman Catholic and Armenian
cemeteries, where Mrs. Sladen and several
other Europeans were already buried. It was
afterwards enclosed and raised by means of
funds supplied by the British Government,
and it was consecrated by Bishop Milman on
his first visit to Mandalay.

The King said that the schools, both for
boarders and day-scholars, would be built and
maintained at his expense ; that they would
be erected according to the Burmese pattern,
with such alterations as I might require.

With regard to the Church he asked me to
give him the plans, and he would build it at

his own cost. I mentioned that friends in
Rangoon, Calcutta and England would gladly
contribute towards the expense. The King
looked proudly at me and said : " *Nga min
bè !* " " I am a King, I want no assistance
in my works of merit," for such he deemed
the erection of church and schools. The only
contribution that he allowed was that of Her
Most Gracious Majesty Queen Victoria, who,
when she heard of King Mindôn's liberality,
of her own accord sent out a most beautiful
font of variegated marbles, in token of her
appreciation of the King's kindness.

It was through my colleague, the Rev. J.
Trew, that Queen Victoria came to hear of
King Mindôn's liberality to us at Mandalay.
While he was home on furlough, and preaching
on behalf of the Society for the Propagation of
the Gospel before the Queen at Whippingham,
he told the story of the Mission at Mandalay,
and the Queen was at once interested.

While I am speaking about Queen Victoria,
I will tell another story which concerns her
and King Mindôn. When the school in Mandalay was in full working order, and the
King's sons were pupils in it, a general holiday

was given on the occasion of the birthday of Queen Victoria.

The King, finding that the young princes were at home instead of being in school, sent for me and asked me what the school was closed for. I replied that it was the 24th of May, and that day, being the English Queen's birthday, was usually observed as a holiday in all the best English schools

The King thought for a moment, and then said: "But why don't you give a holiday on my birthday?" "Because," I replied, "I am unaware of the date of your Majesty's birth. If you will tell me the date I will gladly give a holiday." "My birthday," replied the King, "is Tuesday, every Tuesday!"

The school was to be for a thousand boys. The King asked me when it was ready if I would undertake the English education of some of his sons. Of course I replied that I would most gladly do so. "What age would be suitable for the princes to come to school?" I suggested from twelve to fourteen as a good age. He turned to one of his servants and said: "Bring to my presence all my royal sons who are about twelve or fourteen years old." Nine boys were produced. His Majesty had a very large family, and laughed heartily at me when I asked him the total number of his sons and daughters. He had 110 children !

The King asked me if I could procure him machinery and other merchandise. I told him distinctly that I had nothing to do with politics or commerce—being simply a religious teacher, and as such earnestly desirous to serve the King and his people. My answer seemed to please him at the time, but the proposal was afterwards again and again made to me.

When the interview had lasted about two hours, the King concluded it by inviting my boys and myself to breakfast in the Palace for the following day, and by accepting the beautifully bound books which the Calcutta S.P G. Committee had sent as my present.

The next day we went, as commanded, to the Palace , Major Sladen was too poorly to accompany us. My boys were Moung Gyi (now a most respectable well-to-do merchant) ; Moung Ba Tu (now an Extra-Assistant Commissioner and K.S.M , the highest provincial title of honour) ; Moung Ba Ohn (now barrister-at-law in good practice in the English Courts

From a contemporary print.] [By kind permission of the Society for the Propagation of the Gospel.

Dr. Marks and Pupils before King Mindon.

[Facing p. 172.

in Upper Burma); Moung Tsan Hla Oung
(an Arakanese, now schoolmaster in Akyab);
and Moung Po Ming, who died some years ago.
The King was magnificently dressed, and had
the order of the Tsalwè of twenty-four strands
of gold crossed over his breast, and he was
adorned with beautiful rubies, diamonds and
sapphires. Several of the queens and prin-
cesses were with him. He was more stately
and ceremonious than on the previous day,
but equally kind and pleasant.

My boys prostrated themselves, as did the other
Burmans, whilst I squatted down in a cramped
position, being obliged to keep my feet out of
sight. The King was seated on the highest
of a flight of six steps. He began by asking
if I was comfortably housed and cared for.
He reiterated his promises of the day before,
and expressed his hope that all would not be
in vain. He made me tell him about each boy,
and he addressed some kind words to them.
I presented him with a telescope, and the boys
gave a lot of English toys to the young princes.
In return the King gave two *putsoes*, valued
at £3, to each boy. I also presented to the chief
Queen, through His Majesty, a box of beautiful

needle and crochet work made and presented by the Burmese girls in Miss Cooke's school. The King pulled out two or three pieces of work, but did not seem to know much about them. He tossed them to the ladies behind him, who evidently valued them highly.

The King began to talk to the boys about religion. He told them that they should not lightly forsake their ancestors' creed. I interposed, when he laughingly said : " Oh, *Hpôn-daw-gyi* " (" high *Hpôngyi*," the name he always gave me), " I and you will talk about these matters alone by ourselves." I replied that I should be delighted to converse with His Majesty on those subjects, which were of the highest moment to all mankind. The King said that he only wanted to guard the boys against being rash and foolish, or changing their religion to please men ; that he was perfectly tolerant ; that he had never invited a Mussulman, Hindu, or Christian to become a Buddhist, but that he wished all to worship according to their own way.

He told me to make what use I pleased of his steamers between Mandalay and Rangoon, and to grant passages to and fro to any boys whom I might wish to send. We were then conducted to another apartment, where a sumptuous breakfast was served to us in English style. My boys and I sat down to table, the Burman attendants wondering to see our lads freely using knives and forks instead of the orthodox fingers in eating. Suddenly my boys all slipped off their chairs on to the ground, and when I looked up to see the cause, I found that one of the elder princes, a lad of about seventeen, had entered, having been deputed by his father to see that all was right.

Next morning I went again to the Palace with my boys, to take the plans for the school and teachers' residence. He approved of the plan with one exception, viz., that the school must not have a triple roof, such being only for princes and *Hpôngyis*. My house is to be so honoured. The King's Minister for Public Works was called into the presence and ordered at once to commence the work, and to use all expedition in its completion. The King gave me £100 towards school furniture. I told him that I would procure a plan in Rangoon for the church. He repeated that it would

trouble him very much if no English *Hpôngyi*
came to Mandalay. I assured him that his
liberality would not be so despised, but that
I really would return myself and open the
school.

After some further general conversation the
King spoke to the boys, and especially to the
Arakanese boy whom I had adopted in 1863.
He repeated what he had said before about not
forgetting the religion of his ancestors. I
said that the boy's ancestors had not heard the
good news which I taught him. The King
took no notice of what I said, but continued
to the boy, " Always remember the *Yittana thôn
ba* (the three objects of devotion), the *Paya*
(Buddha), *Taya* (law), and *Thinga* (clergy)."
I said : " Christianity teaches us to worship
the everlasting God, to obey His law, and to
receive instruction from the clergy." The
King seemed annoyed for a time, and then
repeated in his usual good-humoured manner :
" I cannot talk with you about religion in
public, we will talk about it privately on your
return." He added : " Do not think me an
enemy to your religion. If I had been I
should not have called you to my royal city

If, when you have taught people, they enter into your belief, they have my full permission;" and then, speaking very earnestly: "If my own sons, under your instruction, wish to become Christians, I will let them do so. I will not be angry with them."

The *Kalawun* told the King that he had heard me pray for the health, happiness and prosperity of the Burmese King and the royal family in our service on the previous Sunday. I gave him a copy of the prayer for himself and for our Queen Empress in the vernacular, and also the Confession and other parts of the Prayer Book. He read several portions aloud, and seemed to be deeply interested.

I had two further interviews with the King on the 30th and 31st of October. I went to the Palace with my boys on Friday, October 30th. After repeating what he had said before, His Majesty asked whether we had *mè thila yin* (nuns) like the Roman Catholics. He said that he thought that some English ladies would be very useful in Mandalay, and that he would give all possible help in their work.

I replied that we felt it better not to begin

too many things at once, but that when our
church, boys' school and residences were built,
we should be delighted to further His Majesty's
wishes to have lady teachers for the prin-
cesses and other girls His Majesty repeated
that it would make him look very foolish in
the eyes of his subjects if, after all he was
doing for us, no missionary were to be sent
to use the church and to teach the boys. I
replied again that everything would be done to
prevent such disappointment.

His Majesty made me come on the following
day to take leave. Accordingly, on Saturday,
the 31st, I took two of my boys to the Palace.
The King assured me that he would hasten
on the work, which would be completed
regardless of expense. He then placed before
me two bags, each containing Rs. 500, one as
a contribution to the work of the Rev. P.
Marks, my brother, who was a missionary in
Ceylon, the other a personal present to myself.

I said that though assured of His Majesty's
goodwill, I would accept no such present.
This refusal was likely to have caused some
unpleasantness. The *Kalawun* earnestly re-
quested me to accept it. So, addressing the

King, I said that it was not the custom of English missionaries to accept such presents for themselves, but that if His Majesty would allow me to be his almoner, I had many ways of using his money so as to do good to others, and I would send an account of all through Captain Sladen.

His Majesty at once assented and entered into a long and pleasant conversation about English schools, books, etc   He wished to have the " Encyclopædia Britannica " translated into Burmese, and he asked me to bring up about fifty of my Rangoon schoolboys for that purpose ! He asked me to leave one or two of my present boys with him, promising that he would take care of them, but no boys wished to stay without me.

We saw the work of building the schools actually begun—the portion of land adjoining the British Residency carefully staked out and surrounded with a royal fence, and on All Saints' Day I solemnly dedicated our cemetery, until it could be properly consecrated, with a short service, to which all Europeans were invited. We left Mandalay on November 2nd, with deep thankfulness to the great King

of kings, who has taught us in His Holy Word
that the hearts of kings are in His rule and
governance, and that He doth dispose and
turn them as seemeth best to His Godly
Wisdom. We stayed a while at Thayetmyo,
Prome, Myan-aung, and Henzada, greatly
cheered by the progress of the work in all
those stations, and by the open door which
presented itself at so many other places.

On returning to Rangoon I had to stay a
while to allow the Rev. C. Warren to go to
Calcutta for his priest's ordination, and Mr.
Chard for deacon's orders. Then Bishop
Milman summoned me to Calcutta to confer
with himself, the Government, and the Calcutta
Committee respecting the new work in Upper
Burma. It was not regarded in India and
Burma with the same enthusiasm as that with
which the news was received in England.
There were not wanting those who utterly
mistrusted the King, disbelieved his promises,
and tried to dissuade me from going up again
lest he should seek occasion to injure me and
the work which he could not love. The
wildest rumours were circulated, amongst
others, that a Burman Christian teacher from

our Myan-aung school had been beheaded for walking in a Mandalay monastery with his shoes on. Telegrams to and from Myan-aung soon assured us that the teacher had never left his station, but was diligently doing his work there. So with many similar rumours.

But these were all quieted when I had the opportunities which the chaplains afforded me of telling the true story in the Rangoon churches, and my friends then came forward willingly with funds and promises of help for the endowment of the work, which all felt should be secured against any possible change of mind of the King, or of a different Government.

CHAPTER XIV

VISIT TO SIR JOHN LAWRENCE

I WENT up to Calcutta and was the guest of Bishop Milman and his devoted sister. I was taken ill on the voyage, and for the first day or two after my arrival was unfit for work. But there was much to be done with regard to the Society's operations and plans both in Upper and British Burma.

My time in Calcutta was fully occupied in earnest consultation with the Bishop and the Rev. J. Cave-Browne, the Secretary of the S.P.G. Committee. The Bishop and Miss Milman had one of their wonderful " At Homes," whereto came Rajahs and Zemindars, and clergy and ladies, native and European, and his Excellency Sir John Lawrence, the Viceroy and Governor-General of India. The Bishop introduced me to him, and after a few minutes' conversation his Excellency invited me to breakfast and talk at Government House on the following day.

Sir John Lawrence was a very homely, kindly, but determined ruler, greatly disliking pomp or show, humble-minded yet decisive in his utterances. Many were the stories that one heard of his simple habits, his love of business, his firm decision as a ruler. One story relating to the Koh-i-noor, the then largest diamond in the world, which was in his custody as Governor-General preparatory to its being sent to Queen Victoria, illustrates his indifference to the pomps and vanities of the world.

The mode of sending the jewel was being debated by the Viceregal Council at Government House, with Sir John presiding. One member asked very pertinently : " Where is it now ? " Sir John said afterwards that his blood ran cold, for he remembered that for several nights it had reposed in the jacket pocket of his pyjama suit, which was at that moment hanging up in the bath-room. Excusing himself for a few minutes, he rushed into the room, and, to his great relief, found it wrapped up in a bit of tissue paper safe in his pocket !

Our breakfast was a very simple meal, and when it was finished, we adjourned to the library, where His Excellency began at once concerning my proposed obedience to the King of Burma's command. He said that he had studied the subject in various aspects, and with the advice of his counsellors, who knew Burma well, he was opposed to the project on political grounds.

The two Burmese wars of 1825 and 1853 had been fearfully expensive in blood and treasure. We had conquered and made a division of the country which, with all its difficulties, he hoped to be permanent. This was the first infraction of the understanding that foreign missionaries should not be sent to Upper Burma, and although the initiative came from the King himself, His Excellency could not divest himself of the feeling that it contained the seeds of future political trouble. He further pointed out the possibilities to myself by instancing the sufferings of Dr. Judson and other American missionaries before the last war.

He acknowledged that King Mindôn was a good monarch, but he pointed out that as a ruler he was a failure in that he was ruling for the people instead of governing them, and so on. With all this I perfectly agreed. " But," I said, " my knowledge of the conditions of Burma convince me that its annexation by us is only a matter of time."

Sir John rose from his chair with more anger than I deemed him capable of, and said : " If you wish to remain a friend of mine, you will never use that hateful word ' annexation ' in my presence again. Let me say, once and for all, we cannot afford to annex Upper Burma. We neither desire it nor are we capable of accomplishing it. Annexation has been the cause of troubles without end. We had a disturbed frontier on the Punjab of forty miles. We therefore went to war, and now we have a disturbed frontier on the Punjab of four hundred miles, and the Indian Mutiny as another consequence.

" The Indian princes and peoples got to distrust us, and all because of the policy of annexation. With all its imperfections, it is desirable that the treaty with Upper Burma should stand. Never let it be so much as whispered that there is any thought of annexation. What we all feel here with regard to your scheme is that the Burmese King, who, with all his excellences and weaknesses, is an astute ruler, wishes to get you into his power for two reasons. One of them is flattering to yourself ; he has heard, as we all know, of your work for Burmese boys in British Burma. He wishes to stop that work because it is antagonistic to the Buddhism of which he is the acknowledged secular head. The other reason is that he wishes to utilize you politically, and if you should not come up to his expectations in this respect, you will be imprisoned or murdered, and we shall have trouble with the Burmese Government, which is just the very thing which we wish to avoid. Don't go."

I replied that I fully appreciated all that His Excellency had said, and that I greatly regretted that I had incautiously used a word which he from his deep experience deprecated. But, with regard to the King's wish, while I acknowledged that such designs might be uncharitably attributed to a Western potentate,

I firmly believed that the invitation or command was an answer to my continued prayer, and that unless obedience to it were rendered impossible, I certainly would obey it. I determined that while I was in Mandalay I would absolutely refrain from all politics, whether secret or open. That as regards personal risks of possible dangers, I entirely disregarded them, for, as I was acting in obedience to God's call, I should be under His protection, and I did not desire any other.

Sir John rested his head between his hands and for some moments was in deep thought. Then, coming to me, he said : " I see that you are determined to go. We will not hinder you. Only distinctly understand this, that you go, not as an envoy of the British Government, but entirely on your own responsibility. With whatever may happen to you we have no concern. If you are imprisoned or get killed in any way, it's of no use your crying out to us to come and help you. We will do nothing of the kind."

I replied : " I assure your Excellency that under those circumstances I will be perfectly quiet !" Sir John burst out laughing. " Go, my dear fellow," he said, " and God's blessing be with you. Only be very careful." Later on in the day he sent me a cheque for Rs. 500 towards expenses.

CHAPTER XV

WORK IN MANDALAY

I RETURNED in better health and spirits to Rangoon, and heard that the King was faithfully fulfilling his promises, and that the schools and my residence would be ready by the time that I could begin work. So with several tame boys and pupil-teachers I set out again for Mandalay.

I left Rangoon on April 6th, 1869. My voyage up the Irrawaddy, accompanied by ten of my best boys from St. John's College, was necessarily slow, as I wished to visit, perhaps for the last time, all my riverine schools.

I inspected the school at Zalun, but by a misunderstanding with the captain, the river steamer failed to call for me, and I had to walk seventeen miles to Henzada. We set out at four o'clock in the morning dressed in our lightest. It was nearing the end of the dry season and about the hottest part of the year. Our path lay along the bank of the river, which was then at its lowest. The ground was hard and seamed with deep fissures through the heat.

We stopped on our way at a large village called Doungyi, where the Burmese magistrate begged me to stay and do what I could for his son, one of my pupils, who was suffering from fever. I gave him some quinine, and I heard with great pleasure afterwards that he had recovered; but we bitterly regretted the delay, for it prolonged our journey into the heat of the day.

We trudged on and on, and there was absolutely no shelter. I never was a good walker and became more and more distressed, but at length we entered the long straggling town of Henzada, where, although the road was now sheltered in parts, I seemed to experience more distress than ever, and at last, more dead than alive, I arrived at the Government Circuit House.

I had barely reached the central room, where my kind friend Colonel Plant was awaiting me with breakfast, when I fell down on the floor, utterly unable to stand. He very wisely and kindly threw a lot of cold water over me and took other measures which restored me to consciousness and some degree of vitality. But my cruel walk inflicted injury upon me from which to this day I have not recovered.

I found that the school was doing well and was full of promise. It required more supervision than I could give it with my multifarious duties, but it was full of promise.

I next went on to Myan-aung, where our school had been established under the patronage of Major Hildebrand. It was well cared for by the Christian residents and was doing well. I then went on to Prome, where I conducted service. At Thayetmyo I called several meetings of the Burmese, and went with two or three of them, and collected in two days over Rs. 600 for the new school. But the exposure to the fierce heat of the sun which I encountered during my canvass in the bazaar, brought on a serious indisposition and I was obliged to return to Prome.

My instructions from the Bishop were that

I was not to proceed to Mandalay until I heard from Major Sladen that the buildings were sufficiently advanced. I therefore remained at Prome and acted as chaplain of that place until June 2nd, when, hearing satisfactory news from Major Sladen, I proceeded on my journey to Mandalay where I arrived on June 7th, 1869.

After a few days' stay at the Residency, I removed into the grand Clergy House (or *Hpôngyi Kyoung*) which the King had built for me, and as soon as possible we opened the S.P.G. Royal School for boarders and day-scholars of several nationalities. I had several very interesting interviews in public and private with the King, whose kindness was very great. At one of these he again asked me to receive his sons as pupils at our school. I replied that I should be delighted. They came, very grandly dressed, and kneeled down before their father, who said to me, " I deliver them over to you."

They appeared to be very bright and intelligent lads, and I willingly accepted the trust. But knowing the punctilious etiquette of Burmese royalty, I ventured to suggest that nine princes would be too great an honour to begin with, and that I should prefer to commence with four The King consented, and on the following Monday morning the Shwé Koo, Mine Done, Thibaw and Thagara Princes came to school. One of my Rangoon pupils rushed into my room and said : " Teacher, the princes are coming." I looked out, and there were the four princes, mounted on four royal elephants, two gold umbrellas held over each, and forty followers in "undress uniform" behind each elephant. The long procession came up to my door ; the elephants knelt down, and the princes descended and came up into my room. I had prepared a lot of mechanical toys, telescopes, etc., for the entertainment of the princes. But their followers rushed up, pulled off the table cover, and threw it and all my pretty things into the corner, and put the princes' spittoons and waterpots on the table.

I suggested that we had better cross over to the school hall On our arrival we found twenty-five boys seated at their desks. But as soon as the princes entered every boy, according to Burmese custom, went down flat on the floor—none dare stand or sit in the presence of royalty. I said: " Boys, get up to your desks. The princes have come here not as King's sons (*min thas*) but as scholars " (*kyoung thas*, literally " sons of the school "). But though I repeated this three or four times no boy moved. At length I went forward and pulled up one boy, who looked very miserable and frightened. As soon as I released him to raise up number two, he went down flat upon his face again—worse than at first. It was, of course, impossible for me to teach pupils in that position, and I was greatly perplexed. But turning round to the princes, I saw that they were shaking with laughter. So I said: " Please tell those boys to get up and go on with their work." The eldest, the Shwé Koo Prince, said : " Oh, you fellows, you are not to be frightened at us. We are your school-fellows ; get up, and go on as if we were not here." One by one the boys crept up to their seats. But school worked very stiffly for a day or two, until the boys and teachers got familiar with the royal pupils

Very soon all came right. I have never had more gentle, docile, and intelligent pupils than

were these princes, and I was glad when all
the nine came—though it was more like a procession of Sanger's Circus through the streets
than that of pupils coming to school. It was
the King's express wish that his sons were to
be educated in exactly the same.subjects and
in the same way as the other pupils were
being taught. Especially he desired that they
should be instructed in our Holy Religion,
that they should consider and decide when they
came to a proper age which was the better—
Buddhism or Christianity. In accordance with
our invariable custom in all our S.P G. Mission
schools, every day's work was begun with
prayer for God's blessing, and to every pupil
every day, instruction in the Christian religion
was given as he was able to bear it. The
King was particularly interested in this subject, and liked to see day by day his sons'
Scripture lessons, which were very often the
subject of conversation when I went to the
Palace, which, at the King's request, I did very
frequently. To facilitate my visits he bought
for me a beautiful carriage (technically called
a Madras Nibs), drawn by two trotting bullocks. But I had many a weary waiting in

the Palace, where there were no chairs, and the only seats were folds of carpet on the floor. After hours of this posture my limbs ached, and I was fit for very little on my return to the Clergy House.

Major Sladen, just before proceeding on leave on account of his health, took a photograph of our school, which showed the four *Ko daws* (princes).

We played cricket on Thursdays and Saturdays, and the young princes entered very heartily into the game.

I must here tell one characteristic anecdote of His Majesty. Shortly after the princes came to school, the King asked me whether I would allow them to be absent on the days of Buddhist worship—*i.e.*, the New Moon, the 8th waxing, the Full Moon, and the 8th waning day. I replied that it was not the custom of our Mission schools to recognize these days, and that as a Christian *Hpôngyi* I could not sanction any of my pupils' absence on those days; but that still it was competent for His Majesty, as a father, to keep his sons from school whenever he chose. The King replied: " Quite right. I know that you wish to teach my sons what is good. I wanted you to recognize my right to keep them away when I desire, but you will have no cause to complain of their irregularity."

The other pupils from the Palace were called *Lapet ye daw thas—i.e.,* sons of tea—because they hand tea to the King. They were entitled to a yellow silk umbrella, and each had a dozen or so of followers. Most of them were over twenty, and married ! The King ordered them to school, and they came when they could find no plausible excuse for staying away. They naturally found their family arrangements incompatible with their scholastic duties. Still, some of them made good progress, and in school they were, like all Burmese boys, excellent pupils.

Both in Mandalay and in Rangoon I often had married men as schoolboys. I remember once seeing a big schoolboy bullying a small boy in the school playground. I called them both up into my house, and, without waiting for any explanation, immediately administered a sound thrashing to the big boy. After I had finished, I said : " Do you know why I have beaten you ? "

He replied : " No."

I said : " It is time that you understood that I do not allow big boys to bully small ones in my school."

The big boy gave a sickly smile and replied : " Please, sir, he is my son ! "

It was a pretty sight to see the boys come to school. Some came on richly-dressed ponies, some in beautifully carved little carts drawn by trotting bullocks, some on elephants, and some on men's shoulders. We had a large bell, weighing 360 lbs., cast in the Palace. In the compound there was a special building called the *Ane daw*, or royal house, where the princes spent the recess from twelve to one daily.

CHAPTER XVI

CONSECRATION OF MANDALAY CHURCH

THE King was in haste to redeem his promise to build the church. I could not get plans. But I had old numbers of the *Illustrated London News*, containing a picture of the new chapel of St. John's College, Cambridge, and with the help of this I pieced together a picture of a church that I thought would be suitable, and a friend in the Public Works Department in Rangoon drew working plans. We got the posts into the ground—grand teak pillars—when Bishop Milman and his chaplain, the Rev. A. O. Hardy,* came up.

The church was not ready for consecration, but the Bishop approved of our plans, and solemnly dedicated all our buildings, and

* *Cf.* Letters 3–9.

examined our scholars, the princes included, and awarded prizes. His lordship held a Confirmation in the pretty little Oratory of the Clergy House, and consecrated our cemetery. The latter was a work of some difficulty, for the waters of the Irrawaddy were out, and the road to the place, and the land itself, were submerged. We had to wade to the spot, and we had to walk round on the low wall of the cemetery, there being a couple of feet of water on each side! We were much cheered by the Bishop's visit, and went on heartily with the church building.

I should have mentioned that on September 1st, at the request of the Lord Bishop, conveyed through me, and in the presence of three of the King's sons, the Armenian priest, and of all the principal European residents and many Burmese officials, Major E. B. Sladen, the British Political Agent, with Captain G. Strover, Assistant Political Agent, publicly laid the foundation-stone of the church. The *Kalawun*, specially deputed by the King, said: " I beg to assure you that the spot on which we are now assembled is part of the land which is publicly

given by His Majesty the King of Burma
for the purposes of religion and education in
connection with the Church of England, and
also that His Majesty has promised to defray
all the expenses of the erection of this church,
as he has already paid for the building of the
English Christian School and Clergy House."

The Bishop came up again next year (1873)
with his chaplain, the Rev. Edgar Jacob
(afterwards Lord Bishop of St. Albans), for
the consecration of the church.

They arrived on July 25th, and the King
sent for me at once to inquire whether the
Bishop was well, and if he was satisfied with
the church and schools. Having reassured
him on this point, it was arranged that the
Bishop should visit the Palace on the following Monday. On that day the Bishop, Mr.
Jacob, the Bishop's doctor, and some of my
elder boys, went to the Palace, and were met
at the bottom of the stairs by the Mine Done
prince, who, having met the Bishop on his
previous visit, and speaking a little English,
was deputed to conduct his lordship to the
audience hall.

We had scarcely arranged ourselves com-

fortably, when the doors were thrown open
and the King, beautifully dressed and attended by three or four little children, walked
in and threw himself on a couch at the raised
part of the room. He took up his binoculars
and had a good look at the Bishop. The usual
questions were asked as to the Bishop's age,
and the King laughed to find that he was
younger than himself.

The Bishop then earnestly thanked His
Majesty for the beautiful church, school and
clergy house which he had built.

His Majesty replied that he could not help
doing what I asked him, that he loved me as
if I were his own son, and that the Bishop
must not change me for any other *Hpôngyi*.
But yet, that I was too haughty and im-
patient !

His Majesty then spoke of his earnest wish
for the continuance and increase of friendliness
between his country and the English Government, and many compliments passed between
the King and the Bishop on this head, who
promised to tell Lord Northbrook all that the
King said, assuring His Majesty that his
pacific and friendly sentiments would be

cordially reciprocated by the Governor-General. The conversation was in danger of becoming political, but the Bishop, with excellent tact, turned it off into other channels.

The King gave his lordship a beautiful ruby ring, which the Bishop would have fain declined, but I begged him to accept it, and by His Majesty's order, I put it on his finger. The King wished to defray all the Bishop's charges till he should reach Calcutta, but this his lordship kindly but firmly declined. Further conversation ensued, when the King, bidding me come privately to him on Wednesday, rose and left us, though not so abruptly as he usually departs on such occasions.

The next day the Bishop and his chaplain held an examination of the school. The boys were quite taken aback when the Bishop commenced. One fainted away, but recovered, and came out second in the school. His lordship sent the following report to the King : " I carefully examined the Royal S.P.G. school, which is a very good school. Its tone and character are high. I have examined most of the schools all over India, and can therefore speak with confidence. The school has improved considerably under its present teacher, Mr. Mackertoom. The number of pupils, ninety-two, is much increased, and those who have grown up and left are likely to be useful members of society. The school is a real benefit to His Majesty's subjects."

The church was consecrated on the 31st of July. Nearly all the European residents in Mandalay, including, besides Englishmen, French, Italians, Armenians and East Indians, were present at the service. The Shwé Koo prince came alone, as his brother, the Mine Done, had an attack of fever, which prevented his coming. The *Kinwun Mingyi*, the head of the embassy which visited England and Europe, came attended by the *Yaw atwin wun*, Minister of the Interior, the *Myo wun*, city magistrate, and the *Kala wun*, representing His Majesty.

The collection at the service amounted to forty pounds, of which I am glad to say the prince gave ten pounds.

Before the prince and the ministers left to report the proceedings to the King, I asked the former how he liked the service. He replied : " It was very good and the singing very pleasant, but it was a long time to be without a cheroot ! " He was a great smoker, and when he was at school got leave every hour for a pull at his cigar. During the service he and the ministers and all heathen Burmans sat in the aisles, according to our rule

After luncheon, when more than forty people sat down, the Bishop chaffed me on the " missionary hardship " of having to live in my beautiful clergy house. I meant to have made a good speech, but I utterly broke down, as my heart was too full at the realization of the fulfilment of a project which had been so frequently and persistently hindered. With regard to my beautiful house, however, I could not help recalling what my friend Dr. Mason, the veteran American Baptist missionary, had said to me—that I was, as it were, occupying a pretty villa on the slope of a volcano !

Soon after this I was joined by an English schoolmaster, who, however, did not stay long, as I preferred to work with my own trained and very efficient assistants, natives of the country, all of whom have done well since in various capacities.

Matters went on very smoothly for a couple of years, and then there gradually came a coolness on the part of the King.* Little difficulties had often arisen from the first, too trivial perhaps for record, but as time went on they gradually increased. The King sent more boys, boarders and day pupils, to the school, but the monthly payments became more and more irregular. Once, when arrears amounted to Rs 500, the King sent only Rs. 200. I sent this back, that I might bring to his personal notice that the work was not being conducted for my private benefit, and that I had none but his funds to maintain the school.

For a few days the King was angry and did not call me. Then he sent for me and was as pleasant as usual. But he said : " You did wrong to send back royal money. If my highest minister had done so, he would have been dragged out of the Palace by the hair of his head." I assured His Majesty that I had no wish to offend him, and that as to the penalty, my baldness would render its infliction in my case an impossibility ! The King laughed heartily and called the queens to enjoy the

* Cf. Letters 17-19.

joke, and at once paid up the arrears. But he hated to pay regularly, and I was compelled to ask him to do so. Then he persistently asked me to get him some guns and rifled cannon, which, of course, I neither could nor would.

At last one day, in a private room, he unfolded a plan by which I could, as he thought, be of great service to him. I was to go to England in his sea-going steamer, the *Tsitkai-yin-byan*, taking with me two or three of the princes, and when I got to London I was to tell Queen Victoria how good he had been, and ask her to give back to his Government Bassein or Rangoon, that he might have a seaport of his own. Of course I pointed out the impossibility of my undertaking anything of the kind. He got very angry, and said hastily : " Then you are of no use to me." But he soon recovered his good temper and talked pleasantly as others came into the room. But I never saw him again. We were heavily in arrears. I went to the Palace, but, on various excuses, could not obtain an audience or any money, and at last the King said that he did not want me any more, and that I had better leave his capital, adding that my life might be in danger if I stayed.

I sent back word that, having come by his invitation, I certainly should not leave except at my appointed time, some eight months later, and I stayed on, and went on with my work. The princes ceased their attendance, though they took every opportunity of sending me kind loving messages and presents. But the school filled with paying pupils, and was really more efficient than when under royal patronage.

I was joined by Mr. James Alfred Colbeck, of St. Augustine's, Canterbury, and he was of wonderful assistance in those days of trouble. Full of zeal, energy, and piety, he worked nobly as a layman, and then as an ordained missionary afterwards in Rangoon, Maulmein and Mandalay, where, after the war in 1883, he was the first priest in charge of our church, and where he died in 1888, leaving a record which must always live in the story of the Church's work in Burma. His noble self-devotion, his unflinching courage and earnest labours, demand a separate history. It is written in the hearts of the people of Burma and of all who knew him. "He rests from his labours and his works do follow him."

I kept on with the work of the school and church, and of visiting pastorally Bhamo and Myingyan. The new Chief Commissioner of Burma, the Hon. Ashley Eden, was by no means favourable to our Mission work. He tried by threats to induce the Calcutta Committee to sell St. John's College for a Government secular High School. I protested indignantly against such a proposal, and the Bishop supported me, and it and the threats had to be withdrawn. His lordship wrote to me, " The Viceroy, Lord Northbrook, has just been in my room with a letter from the Chief Commissioner of Burma, asking me to order you to leave Mandalay, as your life is not safe there. I replied that it is not our custom to recall missionaries from their posts on the first appearance of danger, and that you had my permission to leave whenever you chose to do so."

There was really no danger, and I continued to have no door to my house or guard to my gate, and none made me afraid. At last, at the appointed time, January 25th, 1875, I was relieved by the Rev. John Fairclough, and with many of my pupils I departed in state from the royal city. I could not help saying, as the steamer was leaving and I took a *stern* view of the place, that I would not return to Mandalay until the British flag floated over it! My prophecy was fulfilled when I revisited it ten years afterwards, and preached to the garrison of British regiments in the hall of the royal palace—itself the temporary chapel of the troops.

CHAPTER XVII

THE FIRST BISHOP OF RANGOON

FOR a few weeks I resumed charge of St. John's College, and then, leaving it under the care of the Rev. J. A. Colbeck and Mr. H. W. Wootton, I took my much-needed second furlough to England *via* Calcutta. There I dined with Bishop Milman, who gave me a kind letter to his relative, the Marquis of Salisbury, then Minister of State for India. It was my last meeting with the dear good Bishop, whose noble work for God's Church in India was drawing to a close. He was, as ever, exceedingly kind to me, and spoke of his contemplated retirement and of the need for a Bishop for Burma. I never saw him again. He died at Rawal Pindi just before I returned to Calcutta, March 15th, 1876.

I greatly enjoyed my furlough in England,

and the deputation work for the S.P.G. Everyone was exceedingly kind to me. I had long and pleasant interviews with Lord Salisbury, and I preached in the Oxford University pulpit, and in many other cathedrals and churches. Archbishop Tait gave me a Bible for our College chapel, Brighton College gave the Service books, Liverpool College the organ, and St. Margaret's, Liverpool, the Altar vessels. I was saddened by the news of the death of the Rev. Charles Warren, the devoted missionary to the Karens. He died of over-work at Toungoo, and his wife soon followed him to the grave. The Rev. T. W. Windley then offered himself, and was accepted, for the work as his successor, remaining at his post till 1882, when illness compelled his retirement, to the deep regret of all who knew his devoted and efficient labours.

I returned to Burma early in 1876, taking with me a student from St. Augustine's, who, however, did not stay long in Burma, but has done useful work in New Zealand.

On my return to Rangoon I found the Mission work greatly extended. I resumed charge of the College and Mission—which under the zealous care of Mr. Colbeck had grown considerably.

Boys flocked into the school, which was soon filled to overflowing, and our chapel was too small for our congregation. Although the Government Secular School had been established as " a rival institution," we could not find room for the many applicants for admission. By the help of Government, Sir Rivers Thompson having succeeded as Chief Commissioner, and that of many other friends, I built a *tectum*, or covered play-room, eighty feet by forty feet But before it was half finished I resolved to add ten feet by forty feet, and join it on to our school hall, and to make more dormitories and class-rooms. This we did, and we had a grand opening day at which the Chief Commissioner and all the great people of Rangoon were present. Soon we found the hall inconveniently large, and the chapel far too small. So we shut off the new part, and turned the old hall into a very beautiful chapel, which was duly licensed, and in which we put the handsome font which friends in Buckingham, led by the Rev. C P. Trevelyan, had given to us. This chapel has now again become

213

very much too small for our native Christian congregation, and we are making great efforts to build a proper church or college chapel on land which the Government has given us, as I have before mentioned.

The Right Reverend Dr. Johnson (whom, as Archdeacon of Chester, I had met a few months before in Liverpool), the newly-appointed Metropolitan, very shortly after his arrival in India paid a visit to Burma, examined the College, and held a confirmation in our chapel. He also made new arrangements, some of which I ventured to think were premature though well intended, in the Mission work.

Shortly after his departure we were gladdened by the news that Burma had been created into a separate see, and that a well-known clergyman of the Diocese of Winchester, which had been foremost in aiding the S.P.G. and S.P.C.K. in providing funds for the endowment, had been consecrated as the first Bishop of Rangoon, and was on his way out. It was, indeed, joyful news. Bishop Cotton, in his primary Charge, had urged the necessity for a Bishop of Burma. Bishop Milman, with all his love for the Burmese

and the missionaries, had tried in vain to get
Madras to take our spiritual oversight, and
almost his last words to me were, " Do your
best to get a real Bishop for Burma." Whatever fears we may have entertained with regard
to the prelate first selected, on account of his
age and his previous work, all vanished when
he came among us.

Though sixty years of age, Bishop Jonathan
Holt Titcomb was full of energy and zeal, a
real hard and diligent worker, an excellent administrator, and one of the kindest and most
lovable of men. I very soon became his
private chaplain, and remained so during the
whole of his episcopate in Burma. His house
was next door to St. John's College, and he
visited us daily. He had a class twice a week
of our elder students for Bible study. Whenever we had baptisms of converts he loved to
be present. He preached regularly in our
chapel, and always had private intercession
with our boys before their confirmation.

We had then a large number of Chinese who
desired admission into our Church by Holy
Baptism. The work amongst them began
whilst I was in England, and Mr. Colbeck

very earnestly prepared them. I took up the
work with them on my return. On most
careful inquiry I could discover no base or
unworthy motive amongst them. Not only
did they not ask for money or other such help,
but they regularly subscribed to the chapel,
schools and orphanage—all were well-to-do
tradesmen or artisans. But we felt it our
duty to be cautious, and when we heard of the
Bishop's appointment we resolved to await
his arrival, and, in accordance with the rubric
before the Service for the Baptism of Adults,
to seek his lordship's guidance and sanction.
Nor was the Bishop less guarded and cautious.
He had several private interviews with each
individual candidate and frequent services of
preparation, all with a thoroughly qualified
interpreter.

At length, having fully satisfied himself
and us, and the members of our other Christian
native congregations, of the sincerity of the
candidates, the Bishop publicly baptized over
forty Chinamen on Sunday morning, in the
presence of a large congregation of all nationalities in the pro-cathedral, the Chief Commissioner and several other high officials being

amongst the witnesses. Neither then, nor ever since, by those Chinese Christians, nor by any others whom we missionaries have baptized, has a single case occurred where a convert has asked for pecuniary assistance. On the contrary, they have been our liberal supporters. If the work amongst them so happily begun has not made commensurate progress, the delay must be attributed to lack of missionaries and to other causes of which I may not now speak particularly. We loved our Bishop, and felt that in him we had a zealous colleague, a firm supporter and a kind friend.

CHAPTER XVIII

THIBAW

AMONG the princes who came to the school at Mandalay there is one in particular of whom I must now speak at length, because about this time he became King of Burma. His name was Thibaw. While at our school (he was number twenty-seven !) he was a quiet, inoffensive, docile lad, without any particular vice or virtue to distinguish him from the other boys of his age.

He was obedient and orderly and gave but little trouble. He never presumed for one moment on his position to expect any preferential treatment. True, he had no expectation of coming to the throne, and even if he had, it is exceedingly doubtful if such expectations would have materially altered his attitude, for he was of a modest and trustful disposition, easily influenced for good or for

Mandalay. King Thibaw's Golden Kyaung.

[Facing p. 218.

evil. Unfortunately he was not long enough with us to strengthen the good points of his character. Let me here tell the story of how Thibaw came to the throne.

In accordance with the custom of the country, King Mindôn had four wives who were queens and many other subordinate wives. These latter were chosen where the King wished. If he saw a beautiful girl and admired her, she became his wife. If a tributary prince offered his daughter to the King, she was accepted as a lower wife.

Two at least of King Mindôn's chief queens were his half-sisters. These were the Laungshé princess—who became the mother of King Thibaw—and the Hsin-byu-ma-shin, the notorious queen-mother, whose daughter, Supayalat, married Thibaw, and was the cause of all the troubles which subsequently over-took him. I have often seen these two queens of King Mindôn. What became of the Laungshé princess, the mother of Thibaw, is not known. She seems to have fallen into disgrace and to have lived and died in ob-scurity, which may mean a good deal in a country like Burma.

The Hsin-byu-ma-shin was the chief queen at Mindôn's death. She had three daughters but no son, and all these daughters became Thibaw's wives. They were called, Supayagyi, ı e., the great princess, Supayagalé, or the little princess, and Supayalat, the middle princess.

On his death at the age of sixty-five, after a reign lasting twenty-six years, King Mindôn had no fewer than seventy sons, but he had not named a successor, and the law of primogeniture did not prevail in Burma ; indeed, it could not, as Mr Scott O'Connor has pointed out, in a country where kings marry so many wives.

Thus ıt came about, to quote Mr. Scott O'Connor once more, that " grave issues were involved in the question of the King's health. Should he die, it was certain that a struggle for the throne would take place among his sons. In this struggle many lives would be taken, disorder would ensue, and the country would be plunged ınto the agonies of civil war.

" All these things had happened before in Burmese history. But it was unlikely that they would be suffered, without interruption, to occur again ; for across the frontier lay a province of the British Empire, and the British Empire was tired of the vanities and pretensions of the Burmese Court. . . The issue of the King's illness was awaited with anxiety—amongst others, by a handful of Englishmen at the royal capital, whose very existence was likely to depend on the turn that events might take.

" One of them, writing in September, 1878, gives a graphic account of the situation. ' I am expecting and watching,' he says, ' for the arrival of refugee princes escaping from an expected massacre. We do not know whether the King is alive or dead, and expect to hear wild outbursts of confusion every moment.' . . .

" The Queen won over the ministers, and it only remained to secure by some signal act of treachery the persons of all the rival candidates to the throne. They were summoned accordingly on the 12th of September, 1878, to visit the King in his chamber. Believing the order to emanate from him they came. Immediately on entering the Palace they were seized and thrown into prison."

Two only of the princes ultimately suc-

ceeded in escaping, and my colleague, the Rev.
James Colbeck, was instrumental in saving
their lives. He has left the following account
of what took place : " A lady of the Palace
came to me dressed as a bazaar woman, and
shortly after, about a dozen others came. I
had to take them in and secrete them as well
as possible. A few minutes afterwards there
came in a common coolie, as I thought.

" I got up and said : ' Who are you ? '

" He said : ' I am Prince Nyoung-yan ;
save me.'

" He was terribly agitated and escaped from
a house in which he was confined, and his uncle
had been cut down—not killed—in opening a
way for the prince to escape. So soon as dusk
came we dressed up our prince as a Tamil
servant and smuggled him into the Residency
compound, right under the noses of the Burmese guard at the gate. He carried a lamp
and held an umbrella over me, as it was rain-
ing, and I spoke to him as a servant until the
coast was clear."

For a few months after the death of his
father, Thibaw reigned peaceably, and a mani-
festo was issued that he was to govern by

means of a council, and that all monopolies
were to be abolished. But when he heard of
the British disaster at Isandhalwana, Thibaw
thought that there was no longer cause to
fear Great Britain, and he proceeded to put
out of the way all possible and probable rivals.
In a few days eighty-six of his blood relations
were either battered or choked to death or
buried alive, and a large number of their
friends perished with them. The *Hpoung
Wun* was the chief agent of the massacre and
he revelled in dashing young children against
the wall and committing other barbarities in
the presence of Thibaw and Supayalat, who
heartily applauded.

Supayalat was the instigator of this and the
subsequent atrocities which marred the reign.
As a child I had known her to be cruel and
vindictive. Her mother knew of her weakness, and instead of correcting it she condoned
it. Talking to me one day about her, she
said: " Yes, she is a bad boy. She has
always been a bad boy," using the masculine
gender as a term of endearment. As far as I
was able to judge, it seemed to me that the
mother's idea was that by encouraging her

in her badness her daughter would acquire
" authority " (*awza*).

Supayalat, as a child, used to catch birds
and then tear them limb from limb in mere
wanton cruelty. It was her way of enjoying
herself.

Such was the character and disposition of
the young girl who, by the connivance of her
mother, and in fulfilment of her own ambitions, became Queen of Burma Her husband
came straight from a monastery to the throne.
He had so distinguished himself in his priestly
studies that his father, King Mindôn, at one
time thought that he was going to be the future
Buddha (*Payaloung*). He left the seclusion
and the discipline of the cloister to assume
the unrestrained and limitless powers of an
absolute sovereign. Could any worse training
be imagined for a king than this ?

After the first massacres Mr. Colbeck still
remained at his post in charge of the Mandalay
Mission ; but at length he was compelled to
leave, much against his will, together with all
the English community, by the withdrawal
of the Political Agent and his staff. Mr.
St. Barbe refused Colbeck's appeal to be allowed

to stay behind on the ground that even if he had the right to risk his own life, he had none to risk compromising the British Government and thwarting the policy in pursuance of which the Resident's departure had been ordered.

After Colbeck's departure, I felt very anxious about the buildings connected with the Mission in Mandalay, and I determined to go myself to see if my personal influence upon my former pupil, King Thibaw, would restrain him from the evil course which he had entered upon, and also avail to protect the buildings which his father had erected for me.

I had already once before attempted this, immediately on Thibaw's* accession, but the previous Resident, Mr. Shaw, represented to the Chief Commissioner, Mr. Aitchison, that my visit might interfere with his (Mr. Shaw's) influence.

Now that there was no longer a British Resident, there could be no question of inter-fering with anybody's influence, so I deter-mined to make another attempt. I resolved to go to Mandalay for a few days to show that

* Cf. Letters 21-23.

the Church of England had not abandoned the church and Mission premises, and that our occupancy did not necessarily follow that of the Political Agency.

If I saw any danger of desecration, I resolved to bring away the altar and the font, and if there appeared to be none, to leave a catechist in charge till better times.

I felt it right that my visit should be public and open, and, therefore, I wrote to the King and Prime Minister a short note, simply saying that as there was no clergyman in Mandalay, I would go for a few days at the end of the month.

I received no reply, and doubting whether the letter had been delivered, I telegraphed to the Kinwun Mingyi, and he replied, asking me to postpone my departure. On the same day I received private information from some of my boys that a Mandalay spy had sent word to the Court that I was going as a spy of the British Government. I therefore sent another telegram, assuring the Kinwun Mingyi that my visit had nothing of a political nature about it, and even proceeded as far as Prome on my journey to Mandalay ; but I was met there with the reply that I should on no account be allowed to visit Mandalay for the present, and that if I persisted, orders would be issued to prevent my crossing the boundary.

After this I made no further attempt to visit Mandalay in Thibaw's time, but some years afterwards, in 1886, when the Burmese kingdom had come to an end, I was allowed to visit the queen dowager and her daughter Supayagyi, when they were in captivity in Tavoy. The Queen spoke very kindly of the days when she had known me at Mandalay, when the princes were under my care. She confirmed the reports that I had often heard, that King Thibaw frequently inquired after me, and expressed surprise that I had never visited him after his accession. He evidently did not know of the Kinwun Mingyi's threat which stopped me on my way to Mandalay in 1879.

I need not detail the events which led to the last Burmese war in 1885. Sir Harry Prendergast led what was not inaptly called "a military picnic" up the Irrawaddy, meeting with little or no opposition. King Thibaw had been kept in a fool's paradise with lying reports by those who were working his ruin.

The old Queen assured me that until he heard the cannonading at Myingyan, the King had no idea that hostilities had commenced. Mandalay, Thibaw, and the army capitulated at once—only too quickly for our rulers. We took Mandalay long before we knew what we were going to do with it. The army, only partially disbanded, was allowed to go off as the men chose. No effort was made to intern them, to enlist them under the British flag, or to give them work. And so, without employment, pay or control, they naturally took to dacoity, and became the nucleus of bands of robbers, which kept the country in a disturbed state for many years.

The Rev. James A. Colbeck thus describes the last hours of Thibaw's dynasty :

" General Prendergast gave King Thibaw one day to consider whether he would surrender himself, his capital, kingdom, and army, or fight Next day the same thrilling scene took place as was witnessed the day before—thousands of men within gunshot of each other. The appointed time expired, and the order was given ' Load ! ' But the officers felt it would be a simple massacre of the

Burmans, and did not say 'Fire!' The suspense was awful. Then at the most critical moment another flag of truce appeared, and Burmese officers of state came to say that the King accepted the terms of peace and would give himself up. The Burmese army was disarmed, and our soldiers proceeded to Mandalay.

"General Prendergast and Colonel Sladen went into the Palace, and found all in confusion. The attendants of the King and queens were engaged pillaging the treasures, gold, rubies, and beautiful silks, and destroying mirrors, lamps, costly carvings and curiosities, which people at home would give much to see.

"Colonel Sladen slept one night in the Palace, near the King, to protect him, and a guard of our men was placed at the gates. Next day the General came and gave Thibaw ten minutes to get ready to leave his country. It took, however, three-quarters of an hour. Then a procession formed · the British flag, the General and his staff, the King, holding his two wives, one by each hand, the queen-mother, Colonel Sladen, then a crowd of ministers of the court, maids-of-honour, British officers, and others, which moved past the great throne, down the Palace steps, through a long lane of our soldiers presenting arms, with fixed bayonets ; and so on till the King and his party were got into bullock-carts and taken under strong guard to the steamer *Thooria*, which was waiting to receive him. The people of the city at first seemed bewildered ; then, as they realized what was taking place, many burst into tears and threw themselves sobbing on the ground, bewailing the loss of their master, cruel though he had been."

One of the first exploits of the British Government in the newly-annexed kingdom was the construction of a narrow gauge railway between Rangoon and Mandalay viâ Toungoo. This work was pushed on with almost American rapidity, and in spite of cholera, dysentery, dacoits and other difficulties, it was ready for opening early in 1889. I was one of the forty gentlemen who left Rangoon by the special train on the evening of February 25th to be present in Mandalay for the ceremonial opening. After the ceremony was finished, I went off to my old residence. But so utterly had the place changed from the Mandalay that I had left fourteen years before that I actually lost my way, and it was not without difficulty and adventure that I at last got to the place.

The deep and rapid stream, the Shwéda Kyoung, upon which my boys and I used to row in our doubled-banked twelve-oared boat in front of the school, had become a miserable little ditch. The royal fence which marked our Mission as a royal foundation, had given way to a light railing, and the British Residency looked seedy and dilapidated.

After service in the church I walked to the cemetery to visit the grave of dear James Colbeck. I could not help recalling the time when Bishop Milman, Captain Sladen and I, with several others, went to consecrate the little corner that the Roman Catholics gave us for our cemetery. We had to wade part of the way, be poled in rafts the other part, and walk the remainder, and the consecration service was read from the top of the unfinished wall, which had two or three feet of water on either side. Every Sunday morning after service, while we were together, James Colbeck and I used to walk to the cemetery to see that it was properly cared for.

On Sunday we had parade service for the

English troops and others in the *Hman-nan-daw*, the grand front hall of the royal Palace. Here in this golden apartment, in which I had so often walked barefoot and anxious, waiting for hours for the appearance of one of my prince pupils with the joyful words, "*Kaw daw mu thi*" ('The King calls you"), I now stood with my back to the throne and preached to a large and attentive congregation. In my long intervals of waiting, in days gone by, I often used to think of the various useful purposes to which the different halls of the Palace might be put. But my wildest flights of imagination never assigned a purpose as that to which we were adapting the hall of audience, that of a military chapel for the British garrison!

CHAPTER XIX

LAST DAYS IN MAULMEIN

UNDER Bishop Titcomb the work of the Church in British Burma made excellent progress. He established the Rangoon Additional Clergy Society, and made his influence felt all over the huge diocese. He took special interest in the S.P.G. Orphan Home, which he aided munificently, and at his recommendation it was called the Diocesan Orphanage for Boys. He frequently invited our orphans to garden parties at Bishop's Court, where the ladies of his family, his efficient coadjutors in every good work, most kindly entertained them.

The accident by which Burma was deprived of his services caused us the greatest sorrow. The roadway on the side of a Karen hill on which he was walking gave way under him,

233

and he fell some twenty feet, injuring his spine, and necessitating his ultimate retirement from Burma, to our deep regret. His name will always be revered and loved in the diocese. His successor was the Right Reverend Bishop Strachan, M.D., who from 1863 had been one of the most prominent of the S.P.G. missionaries in Madras Diocese. It was during his episcopate that Upper Burma was annexed to the British Crown, and the whole country, by leaps and bounds, began to advance in material prosperity, so that now Burma is the largest territorially, and the most prosperous financially, of all the provinces of our great Indian Empire.

After fifteen years' absence I visited England again in 1890, bringing with me two of our students from St. John's College, who, with myself, were most kindly received by bishops and clergy and other friends whenever I had the pleasure of going on deputation for S.P.G. Especially did Archbishop Benson take a most kindly interest in these youths, who in a short time were called to the Bar of the Inner Temple, and are now practising as barristers in Burma. The dear Archbishop, whom I had known in Lincoln in 1875, gave me a beautiful large Prayer Book for our chapel, and in many other ways showed his kind interest in our work. It was during this visit that I was so fortunate as to secure as assistant and coadjutor my dear friend, the Rev. Bernard Mahon, the son of the highly-respected Vicar of Leigh-on-Mendip and S.P.G. Diocesan Secretary. His expenses were paid by a noble lady who heard my appeal for help in Westminster Abbey. Of how great value his services to the College and Mission have been all are aware who know Rangoon.

I returned, after six months' absence, with renewed energy, but with failing powers. Every month told me that a great institution like St. John's College needed a younger and stronger man at its head. Frequent illnesses interrupted my work—although my visits as chaplain to Tavoy and Mergui usually reinvigorated me.

All our institutions were in full activity. The College Cadet Corps in connection with the Rangoon Volunteer Rifles was instituted in the time of Bishop Titcomb, and received the high commendation of Lord Roberts,

General Sir George Chesney, and others. The Orphanage had over a hundred boys, but was a source of deep anxiety financially.

The College had a band of excellent workers—"Shway Yoe," C. I. E., Messrs. W. B. Rutledge, W. B. Tydd, W. Wemyss, R. H. St. John, J. Courtenay, Ko Shwé Hman, and others—to whom its prosperity and success must be ascribed and my heartiest thanks ever be given. I must also mention the excellent work of the late Rev A. Salmon, my *locum tenens* in 1890. "Shway Yoe" (now Sir James George Scott) was head-master in Bishop Titcomb's time, and left us to become H.B.M.'s Resident at Bangkok. He was a man who would adorn any station, and as our head-master, our leader in all that was athletic and manly, we honoured and loved him then, and we shall never cease to regard him with admiration and affection. He did the school great good by infusing or evoking among the boys the athletic spirit which has never since died out.

In 1895 I was stricken with severe illness, heart complaint in a very painful form rendering any exertion difficult and dangerous. I was ordered to England, and feared that my work was done. The Society's Honorary Consulting Physician, Dr. Ogle, confirmed my fears. After a short time, however, I seemed to recover, and went on deputation again, but though I earnestly wished to return to Burma, I had grave doubts whether I ought to resume the care of St. John's College. With the consent of the Society the question was left to the decision of the Archbishop of Canterbury, whether I should return to St. John's, or accept the chaplaincy of Maulmein (my first love), under the Additional Clergy Society.

After a most kind and patient inquiry at Addington, His Grace decided that I should resign the college and take the chaplaincy in Maulmein, Tavoy and Mergui. I spent two and a half very happy years at Maulmein, with frequent visits to and from my old pupils in other stations. But I felt that I had but little strength even for that lighter work. On Sunday, July 10th, 1898, whilst celebrating Holy Communion in the beautiful St. Matthew's Church, I suddenly became ill, and must have fallen had not my kind friends, Messrs. F. S. Copleston and K. G. Burne, sub-deacons, come to my help and carried me into the vestry.

I was again sent home, loaded with kindness and help from all, especially Surgeon-Colonel Sinclair, C.S.I., and Dr. Pedley and my dear colleagues and pupils of St. John's, an institution which, under the very able and efficient management of Mr. J. T. Best, M.A. (Cantab.), is ful'y maintaining its highest reputation. I was over two years in England, an invalid for the most part of the time, but, when well enough, pleading for the dear S.P.G. From the Society and its officers, especially the Rev. Secretary Prebendary Tucker, I have ever received the utmost kindness, sympathy and consideration, both in Burma and in England, so that my visits to the S.P.G. Office have been among the most pleasant and encouraging episodes of my sojourn at home.

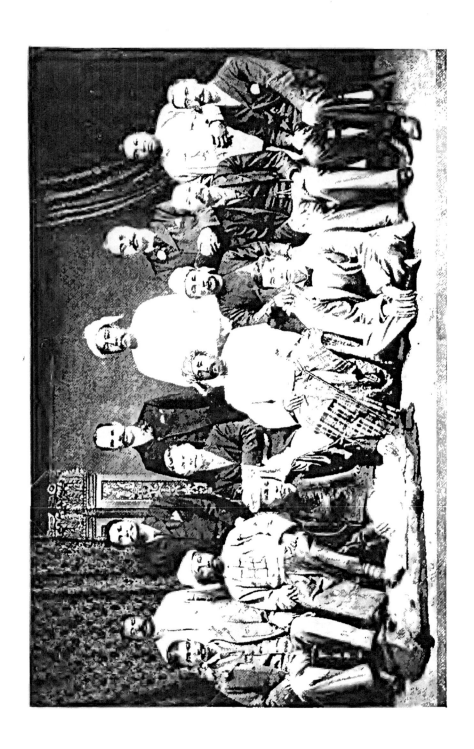

CHAPTER XX

LAST VISIT TO BURMA

WITH returning health and strength my desire to revisit Burma came strongly upon me. A cordial letter of invitation from my "sons" in that country intensified my longing. In August, 1898, shortly after I left Burma, a meeting of my "old boys" was held in the Rangoon Volunteer Head-quarters, at which an Association was formed, called the "Marks' Memorial Fund," with my good successor, J. T. Best, Esq., M.A., Principal of St. John's College, as President ; Mg. Ohn Ghine, A.T.M., C.I.E., Hon. Magistrate, Vice-President ; J. Courtenay, Esq., B.A., Sub-Judicial Service, Secretary ; and Thomas Lyons, Esq., of the Finance Secretariat, Treasurer—(the latter three being my "sons")—with a strong committee of twenty, of whom eighteen were "old boys." It was from this organization that the invitation came, together with a desire to pay all my expenses out there and home.

I very thankfully accepted the invitation thus to revisit my beloved country and my dear "sons" and other friends unofficially, and without any expense either to the Society or to the diocese. I obtained the consent of my good doctors. Messrs. Bibby Bros. kindly made a very substantial reduction in my passage money on the outward journey and several old Burma friends in England contributed most generously towards my outfit, etc.

I took leave of the Society at the monthly meeting on October 19th, 1900, and slipped off quietly to Marseilles, viâ Dover and Calais, on the 22nd. Really, I wanted a few days' rest before embarking, and this I got in pleasant sunny Marseilles—so different from the cold, foggy London which I had left twenty-four hours before, where, indeed, I was being worked too hard. So the entire rest during the four days at Marseilles was very acceptable.

We embarked on board the good Bibby liner *Staffordshire*, 6,005 tons, 4,000 h.-p., on October 27th. On the 10th of November we arrived at Colombo, where our Ceylon fellow-passengers left us. At the Grand Oriental Hotel I had the pleasure to meet the Right Rev. Dr. Pym, Bishop of Mauritius, with whom I dined. Next day I went to Darley House, and spent an hour most pleasantly with the Bishop of Colombo and Mrs. Copleston. I knew the Bishop when he was an undergraduate at Oxford, was with him at St. John's, Oxford, on his last Sunday there, was present at his consecration in Westminster Abbey, and dined with him at Edmonton that night. He most kindly visited me twice on board on my way home. His brother, our Chief Justice in Burma, saved me from falling when I was taken so ill in Maulmein Church, where he was sub-deacon. The Bishop most kindly arranged to take me to my brother, the Rev. P. Marks, Chaplain of Trincomali, on my return journey.

We resumed our voyage on the 15th, and in four days arrived in Rangoon on our twenty-fourth day out from Marseilles. Our steamer

was boarded by a lot of my dear " sons," and
when we got alongside the wharf, Mr. Best,
the Rev. B. Mahon, and others came to give
me a hearty welcome. The wharf was grandly
decorated with flags, and as I landed Burmese
ladies beautifully dressed presented me with
fine bouquets of roses, etc. The following
address was read :

" REVEREND AND DEAR SIR,—On behalf of
the Committee of the Marks' Memorial Fund,
your " sons," pupils and friends have much
pleasure in rendering you a very hearty and
cordial welcome. We have been looking forward to this visit with eager expectation, and
now that our expectation has been realized, we
feel that we have not prayed in vain to meet
you in this, the scene of your former devoted
labours in the cause of education. We hope
that your visit to Burma will be the means of
cementing the ties which have bound you to
us, and we trust that the sunny East during
this delightful weather will restore you to
perfect health again, and that, being filled
with happy reminiscences, you will enjoy your
sojourn among those to whom you have
endeared yourself. You have done for us

more than we can ever repay, but we trust that you will not find us lacking in our efforts to make your visit a happy one.

"Signed on behalf of the Committee and others, J. T. Best, M.A., President; Mg. Ohn Ghine, A.T.M., C.I.E., Vice-President; C. K. Davies, Hon. Secretary, Marks' Memorial Fund."

I replied, heartily thanking all for their kindness and this grand reception, and expressing my intense happiness at being once again in beloved Burma.

A carriage and pair conveyed Mr. Best, M.A., Mg. Ohn Ghine, C.I.E., Moung Shwé Bwin, K.S.M., Judge, and myself. Other carriages, to the number of nearly one hundred, followed. Our guard of honour consisted of over sixty youngsters on bicycles, each bearing a flag of welcome. Immense crowds, larger than I have ever seen on such occasions, greeted us on our way The police kept the road clear for us all the two miles to the College. We halted at appointed places, where Burmese damsels gave us sherbet and other delicacies in golden bowls, and bouquets.

Arrived at St. John's College, we found

flags and arches of welcome and a grandly decorated *mandat*, or tent, beautifully adorned and ornamented. Here an address of welcome was presented to me to which I replied in Burmese, glad to find myself talking that language again—though occasionally stuck for a word, from long disuse.

Then we assembled in the College Chapel, where I returned thanks for God's great mercy in bringing me once more to my dear people. Dinner in the head-master's lodge ended this red-letter day in my life.

The next few days were spent at the College and in paying visits. The Bishop of Rangoon received me most cordially and kindly, as did also His Honour Sir Frederick Fryer, the Lieutenant-Governor of Burma.

On Sunday, the 25th, I preached twice in the College Chapel, which, on both occasions, was well filled with native and European worshippers. In the morning I preached in Burmese on the Gospel for the day, and in the evening in English. I knew from the first that it would be inconvenient for me to stay long at the College. I was its founder and first principal—the only *pucka* one until Mr. Best

came, and my position there might be misunderstood. A constant stream of visitors
interfered with the quiet working of the College. So, with the consent of all concerned,
I took rooms at a club in the heart of the
city, accessible to all at any time, and with
no trouble about housekeeping.

Before I left I went with the Principal all
through the College, and was thoroughly
pleased with the work. It had, of course,
changed considerably since my time. Some
changes I should very likely have made myself. Others rather jarred upon my feelings,
and yet I have no doubt that they had
become necessary by the development of
circumstances. The College was very different
when I gave over charge in 1895 from what it
was in 1864, and one must expect similar
progress in 1901 and hereafter.

I had long and pleasant interviews at his
residence and mine with the Hon. H. Kun
Saing, C.I.E., Sawbwa of Hsipaw, a Shan
potentate, whom I have known under various
circumstances for the last thirty years, and
who was very anxious that we should establish
a Mission amongst his people, the highlanders

of Burma. He had dined with Queen Victoria at Windsor Castle three years previously. His beautiful territory, since the opening of the famous Goteik Bridge, is now accessible by rail from Rangoon. His two sons were in the S.P.G. Royal School, Mandalay, and at St. John's, and came to England with the Rev. George Colbeck, and then went to Rugby. The younger, Saw Khè, the Maington Sawbwa, Regent of Hsipaw, was my dear kind friend in Rangoon, and was, at his own request, photographed with Ko Shwé Hman and myself shortly before I left.

On Sunday, March 17th, against the advice of my good *Medicus* and hostess, I went and preached a short farewell sermon in Burmese at St. John's College Chapel, said " Good-bye " to all the dear people there, and came back very, very tired and went to bed.

On the following day a very large number of friends and myself were taken in a photographic group on Dr. Pedley's lawn.

On March 29th, 1901, I had again to say " Good-bye " to Burma. I was too weak to allow of any very great parting ceremony. I was weary with saying " Good-bye " privately,

Sawbwa Saw Khè, Ko Shwé Hman and Dr. Marks.

[Facing p. 246.

but many old boys came with their carriages to escort me to the wharf. There a very large assembly of all nationalities, of both sexes, and of all ages, came to bid me farewell. A beautiful address was read to me, and a purse of sovereigns handed to me for expenses, my full passage money having been paid. Mr. Best and Mr. Mahon called for three cheers to help me out with my very sorrowful thanks and good-bye.

The Irrawaddy Flotilla kindly placed a steam launch at my disposal to take me to the *S.S. Cheshire*, which at 2 p.m. sailed for England.

I had said " Thank you," from first to last, to all my friends, my " sons, daughters and grandchildren." They asked me on the wharf to promise to return next year. I could not promise, but I would not say " No."

APPENDIX

APPENDIX

A SELECTION OF DR. MARKS' LETTERS AND
REPORTS, REFERRING ESPECIALLY TO THE
BURMESE COURT

LETTER I

To the Rev. the Secretary of the S.P.G.
The British Residency, Mandalay,
Upper Burma, October 20th, 1868.

It is now my duty and pleasure to address you
with regard to my Mission to the King of
Burma. My former letters have put you in
possession of the first stages of the attempt,
but I think that it is better that I should here
recapitulate them.

In 1863 I met in Rangoon the Thōnzai
Prince, one of the sons of the King, who had
fled from the capital I gave him several
Christian books in Burmese, and spoke to him
about their contents. He became reconciled
to the King, and on his return to Mandalay

251

asked me to come and see him at the capital.
He has since sent me several kind messages,
but, as you know, my work and absence in
Calcutta and England left me no leisure to
visit the capital.

After the Bishop of Calcutta's visit last
year, the way seemed open to establish Mission
schools and stations along the Irrawaddy;
and accordingly in two missionary journeys
schools were formed at Zalun, Henzada, Myan-
aung and Thayetmyo.

At this time I received several letters from
Captain E. B. Sladen, the British Political
Agent at the Court of the King of Burma,
telling me of conversations with His Majesty
on the subject of Christianity, and expressing
his belief that a Mission of our Church in Mandalay would not only not be opposed, but
would (under God) effect much good.

One of these letters I forwarded to the Bishop
of Calcutta, who directed me to proceed to
Mandalay with the twofold purpose of minister-
ing to the English residents, and endeavouring
to pave the way for an English Mission.

I met in Rangoon Mr. J. S. Manook, an
Armenian Burman, who is the King's *Kala-*

wun, or minister for foreigners. I told him of our wish to have an S.P.G. Mission in Mandalay, and he promised to lay the matter before the King. Shortly afterwards I received from him the letter, a copy of which I sent you, in which he said His Majesty the King of Burma was pleased at our proposal to establish in Mandalay a Christian school for the benefit of his people, that he would give every possible assistance, and would entrust the children of the officials to us for their education.

I showed the letter to the Chief Commissioner, Colonel Fytche, who was, in 1865, a member of your standing committee, and I sent it to the Bishop. Both agreed that it was an opening of which your Society ought to avail itself, and that I should proceed to Mandalay and there ascertain what could be done. Colonel Fytche furnished me with a letter to the King. It was, however, advised that I should not enter Mandalay until I had heard of the return to that city of Captain Sladen, who had been appointed to lead an exploring expedition to reopen the trade route through Burma to China.

Whilst waiting to hear of the return of

Captain Sladen, I received from the Governor-
General in Council, on the application of
Colonel Fytche, through the Bishop, an appointment as visiting minister of Henzada,
etc. I therefore left Rangoon on the 28th of
August, accompanied by six of my best first-
class boys from Rangoon.

We passed, without stopping, Zalun and
Henzada, and arrived at Myan-aung late on
Saturday evening, the 30th. On the following day I visited the Mission school, which is
under the care of Moung Ba Galé, one of my
pupils from Maulmein and Rangoon, whom I
baptized at the latter place last year. . . .
I next visited Henzada and found that our
school there also was doing well. I also visited
Prome.

The steamer came in on the Monday, and I
left at daylight on Tuesday, arriving at Thayetmyo at two o'clock. At the wharf I was met
by our teacher, Arthur Moung Shway, who
was baptized by Rev. C. A. Berry from our
Rangoon school in 1865, and twenty-seven of
his pupils. I remained in Thayetmyo for a
fortnight, teaching in our school, and endeavouring, by my Sunday help, to repay in

some measure the kindness of the Station
Chaplain, who had most energetically and
effectually maintained our school in efficiency.

We left Thayetmyo on the 1st of October
in the steamer *Lord William Bentinck*, which,
with the flat *Prome* in tow, was crowded with
Burmese passengers. I greatly enjoyed the
voyage as I was passing through country
which I had never seen before. . . .

LETTER 2

To the Rev. the Secretary S P.G.

Clergy House, Mandalay.
June 17th, 1870.

On Wednesday, the 8th of June, I obtained
information that a number of men who had
been concerned in the recent contemplated
rebellion of the Katha Prince were to be publicly beheaded that afternoon in the cemetery
near our Mission compound. My informant
asked me to allow the princes, our pupils, to
leave school earlier on that account, which
I did.

It occurred to me that possibly I might, as a *Hpôngyi*, intercede on their behalf, and I resolved to do so on the consideration that the rebellion had been nipped in the bud, and that no blood had been shed. The King of Burma is firmly seated on his throne ; he has earned a character for mercy such as none of his predecessors enjoyed, and I believed that his power would be still further consolidated by an exhibition of royal clemency.

I intimated to Major McMahon my intention of going to the King, and he reminded me that if I did I must go in my private capacity. I went, therefore, as a Christian clergyman, who has the honour of being known to the King, and who is entrusted with the education of his sons. My colleague, H. Powell, Esq., kindly accompanied me. We walked to the Palace and arrived before the princes. I was advised that if I met the procession on the way to execution, I could, in virtue of my office as a *Hpôngyi*, stop it until the result of my intercession with His Majesty was known, and this I resolved to attempt if I met it, but I did not.

On the princes' arrival they at once informed

APPENDIX

the King that I wished to see him on urgent
business. His Majesty immediately called us
into the *Hman-nan-daw*. The King was
attended by two of the principal queens and
by a large number of officers. He was particularly kind, and inquired what was the
matter, and whether I was still anxious about
the church building not going on so fast as I
could wish.

I began by praising His Majesty's well-
known clemency and humanity, and then
prayed for the lives of the foolish men who
were to be led to execution that day. The
King said that judgment had not been given
and that he knew of no execution. I assured
His Majesty that my information was correct.
The King asked if anyone else knew about it,
and was told by an officer present that there
was to be an execution that afternoon. The
King at once sent him with his royal order
to stop it. I thanked His Majesty earnestly
for his merciful care for the lives of his subjects.
The King replied very kindly, and after a few
moments sent another officer, a *Than daw zin*,
or herald, with the following order: " Go,
stop the men from being led out to execution ;

257   17

and if they have already left, my royal order to the *Myo wun* is that they are to be brought back and not to be killed." . . . On our return we found large numbers of people assembled on the road leading from the Palace to the cemetery waiting to see the procession.

On the following day I obtained from what I must consider an authentic source a list of those who were pardoned on my intercession, and at the head of the list was the name of the Katha Prince himself. I was assured that everything, even to the scarlet velvet bag, was prepared ready for the execution. . . .

LETTER 3

To Bishop Milman of Calcutta.

Clergy House, Mandalay.
July 12th, 1870.

MY LORD BISHOP,

We think it most probable that your Lordship by this time will have reached Thayetmyo en route for Mandalay. I now look forward with real joy to see your Lordship, and I trust and feel sure that your visit will be a real benefit to our infant Mission. I wish that I had cheering news to give, but, alas! after hoping against hope, I am obliged to say that there is no prospect of the church being in any way ready—I did not believe that Burman lying and deceit could have been carried on so persistently. The King arranged that if I would call up a contractor, he would pay out Rs. 5,000 at a time. This again encouraged me that we might push the work on. I was deceived. I have appealed and begged until I have been ashamed, and yet up to the present we have only nine logs in and a few more on the ground, and we have neither timber nor money to go on with. We have here a steam saw-mill, the manager of which would gladly cut timber for me, but we have no wood or money. It is all a mass of chicanery. I do not believe the King himself to be at fault. Our opponent I believe to be Dr. M., who, by making himself useful to the King, has been appointed forest officer, and in that capacity is able to hinder our work.

I remain, your most faithful Servant,

J. E. MARKS.

LETTER 4

To Bishop Milman.

August 19th, 1870.

MY LORD BISHOP,

Since I last wrote to your Lordship,
my brother has arrived, and together we have
visited the Palace three times. On the first
day we went by special invitation, but were
kept waiting outside for an hour and a half,
when we left. No one was there to receive
us, so we returned home. We had scarcely
arrived at the Clergy House when messengers
arrived from the King to express his regret
at the way we had been treated. We returned civil replies, but said that, having
waited so long without seeing anyone in
authority, not even the princes, we had felt
that it was our duty to return home. In the
evening the King sent all the princes to us to
apologize for their neglect in the morning, and

to invite us to come as a special favour on the morrow—Sunday. This, of course, I declined to do, but we agreed to go on Monday. On our arrival we were met by the princes and immediately received by the King, who was remarkably kind and courteous. After some time I delivered your Lordship's message, which H.M. received with evident pleasure, but made no remark except that he said that it was his intention to fill the school with boys from all parts of the country. Yesterday we were again at the Palace. A capital English breakfast had been prepared for us with tables, knives and forks, etc., and the princes sat down with us. It is the King's orders that in future we are to be received in the princes' rooms, where chairs and tables are allowed. The King received us yesterday in perfect privacy, none but the princes, one officer and one of my boys being present, under the tree in the garden house. He talked philosophy, on the value of true friendship, in his desire to get a closer intimacy with my brother and self. This is to be obtained by the interchange of private and confidential letters under seal, in which each is to express himself freely

and without reserve on any point he may wish
to bring to the other's notice, and will bear
" with patience " the other's remarks thereon.
The King is behaving with real kindness to
my brother, though there is no sign of the
books he is to take to Ceylon being ready. All
goes on as usual here. School is filling up
and callers and talkers becoming daily freer
and more numerous. On my return from
Rangoon I hope to commence gradually and
quietly more aggressive work, beginning with
the Kyoungs and parents' houses. The Church
goes on well, though I hope to improve upon
our plans with my brother's aid.

Your faithful Servant,

J. E. MARKS.

LETTER 5

To Bishop Milman.

December 21st, 1870.

MY LORD BISHOP,

Since I last wrote to your Lordship,
I have been to Rangoon. Before I left, I

asked General Fytche privately whether, on my return to Mandalay, I should make any difference in my conduct with regard to the King of Burma's Court pending the decision of Government. General Fytche replied: "Certainly not."

On my return here, the King at first received me coldly. H.M. inquired about your Lordship. He entered again fully into the difficulty which prevented your Lordship's interview, reminding me of what he had said before, that had you consented to come with only the Clergy following, all your wishes should have been complied with, but in the presence of the Political Agent, H.M. could not allow anything which had not been conceded to Generals Phayre and Fytche, who came as ambassadors. He regretted the result, but told me ever to assure your Lordship of his great respect for you and your office. The church had not made much progress: scarcely one of the King's boys were at school, and the school bills were unpaid, including the master's salary. I waited for a fortnight and then solicited another interview with H.M., whom I found as pleasant as ever. I asked what had been the cause of the delays. H.M. replied that I must not think too much of such things, as he had many cares and anxieties which I could not know, but that I was always to be assured of his real interest in my work. The complaints were discussed *seriatim* and all removed. H.M. repeated his intention of sending two hundred boys to the school on my return from Bhamo. He gave me a lot of small coin to distribute on my way up, and placed at my disposal a gilded boat with sixty rowers to take me to the steamer. We arrived at Bhamo on December 1st. A large number of Kachin *sawbwas*, or chiefs, were awaiting the steamer Through a Burmese interpreter I had much conversation with them. They told me, in reply to my inquiries, that they would gladly welcome a Christian teacher. They said that they hoped that such a teacher would protect them from the oppressions of the Burmese, but, of course, I rapidly disabused their minds of any idea of this being a political move.

On returning to Mandalay I was told that during my absence our premises had been watched, and one monk, who had come as usual to visit us, had been marched off to

punishment. On the following day the watch-
man and his attendants were pointed out to
me, and I called them and asked them their
business. They replied that they had been
sent by the *sayadawgyi*, or chief monk, to arrest
any monk who entered our compound, and
that the *Hlut daw*, or High Court, had ratified
the order.

I inquired if they had any written order to
act, and on their replying in the negative, I
said that I had no reason to believe their story,
and as it was contrary to the King's promise
I ordered them to leave the compound, and
threatened to send them to the magistrate if
they came again.

I have been advised to put before you the
points of the controversy between me and
Major McMahon, the British Political Agent.
Neither from your Lordship, the Society, or
General Fytche, have I ever been ordered to
limit my visits to the King or to consult the
Political Agent concerning them. Such directions would have placed me, instead of a missionary, as an agent of the British Government, and an object of distrust to the King.
With regard to the Burmese order of the

Tsalwè, I never asked for or obtained it for myself or others. When the King gave it to two of my present and one of my late pupils, he did it of his own accord. I look forward with patience to a settlement of the matter.

I have the honour to be, My Lord Bishop,
Your obedient faithful Servant,

J. E MARKS.

LETTER 6

To one of the King's Ministers.

January 2nd, 1871.

I received the King's instructions to have the princes and *Lapetyedawthas* taught in the Palace instead of in the Royal School. I am anxious in all things that I possibly can to please H.M., but I do not think that this plan will be good for the princes or *Lapetyedawthas*. They have now been absent from school for more than five months, in which time they have forgotten much that they had learnt. They should be taught by myself or Mr. Powell and not by an under teacher. When we began this school, it was on the understanding that the princes and a very large number of sons would be sent by H.M. Only twenty-five have been sent. We cannot, without the Lord Bishop's permission, daily leave our school to teach in the Palace. I will, however, write to the Bishop and tell him the King's wishes. Meanwhile, I will daily send one of the pupil teachers into the Palace and will come occasionally and see what is done. I can but pray, however, that H.M. will fulfil his royal promise, and send a large number of boys here, and to let the *Lapetyedawthas* come to this school. I ask this for the benefit of H.M. and his subjects.

JOHN E. MARKS

LETTER 7

To Bishop Milman.

Clergy House, Mandalay.
January 21st, 1871.

MY LORD BISHOP,

A short time ago the King called me and said that it was his wish that the princes

and Palace boys should learn in the Palace
instead of going to the city to school ; that
there were state reasons for this, of which he
could not speak particularly. These, I believe,
to be a prophecy by the Brahmins that during
the next few months some great calamity is
impending over him and his family. H.M.
said he would build a school in the Palace,
and that I myself or one of the teachers should
go daily to teach. I replied in a letter that
such a proposal involved a change in the plan
on which the Mission school was founded, and
that I must therefore consult your Lordship.
But that meanwhile I would not object, under
the circumstances, to the princes learning in
the Palace under a pupil teacher, and that I
would supervise their education ; but that I
could not consent to the other Palace boys being
withdrawn. H.M. at once consented, called all
the pages, and insisted on their punctual
attendance at school, threatening that in case
of irregularity he would punish them and
dismiss their parents. School has grown
wonderfully since.

The pupil teachers go daily in turn to the
Palace to teach the princes, bringing their

reports and exercises to me, and I go to see them once or twice a week until your Lordship's orders are received.

I remain . . .

J. E. MARKS.

LETTER 8

To the Rev. F. R. Vallings.

Mandalay.

St. Matthias' Day, 1871.

I greatly regret that the Bishop of Calcutta did not see the King when he was in Mandalay. Despite of all patriotism, I cannot but think that the King was right. If the Bishop came up as he professed in his private capacity, and not as a Government official, the Political Agent would not have insisted in accompanying him to the Palace. The King's argument was this: If the Bishop comes alone—*i.e.*, without the Political Agent—I will accord to him the highest honours accorded to any cleric of my own people. If he comes politically with the Political Agent, I will give him all

I gave to Generals Fytche and Phayre. This, McMahon, acting for the Bishop, declined. The King gave way and said: " Come both and I will do all." McMahon's answer was that it was too late, though they were here six days afterwards! The princes have not been to school here since the Bishop left. There is a farce of a teacher being sent daily, and I go occasionally to see how they are getting on, but it is a farce. The other Palace boys come better, but not in increasing numbers. Meanwhile the school grows from town boys. We have altogether twenty boarders, all of whose expenses are paid by the King, though most of them are Rangoon or Maulmein boys.

You have, I daresay, heard of the unfortunate difference between McMahon and myself, now settled by reference to Council. While my brother was here, McMahon wrote to me to say that he should complain to Fytche of my frequent visits to the King, though I had only been at that time nine times in ten months. I, of course, said: " Do so." On the following day—Sunday—he sent his clerk to tell the Burmese Minister that I was not to be received into the Palace without his consent and this without a word to me on the subject except the one letter. Without knowing of this, my brother and I went to the Palace on the Monday to say good-bye, when we were told of this by the King as a joke. I disbelieved it. The clerk was sent for to repeat his message. The matter then was referred to Fytche, and by him to the Governor-General, and by me to the Bishop. The reply came by last mail that I have no political status, and have nothing to do with McMahon, while yet a Government stipend is assured.

Yours faithfully,

J. E. MARKS.

LETTER 9

To Bishop Milman.

April 13th, 1871.

MY LORD BISHOP,

I have delayed to write to your Lordship in the hope that I might have better news to convey to you in regard to the prospects of the Mission, but I now feel it better at once to let your Lordship know exactly our position and prospects. In spite of his repeated promises, the King has sent no new boys to the school. We have now only eleven Palace boys and about as many others sent with H.M.'s permission. The total number is about seventy.

The princes have not been to school since your Lordship's visit to Mandalay. The King says that there are political reasons why he could not send his sons daily through the city to school, and that though he had sent them at the opening of the school for encouragement, it could not be continued. But he promised to build a school within the Palace where I might live and sleep and teach the princes. I said that such a change in the arrangements could not be made without your permission. I pointed out from the register that the princes had lost more than half of each month, and that they were the most backward pupils in the school.

In a letter to the King, dated the 11th inst., I pointed out that the church was only half finished, and that there was neither funds nor timber to go on with. That the English builder had already, in eleven months, received Rs.2,200, at Rs. 200 per month, and that the dilatoriness in supplying material was adding considerably to the cost. I have had no answer as yet.

Six weeks ago I applied to the King to fulfil his promise to grant us the remaining piece of the compound to the west of the church. The King replied that he had given us a larger piece than the English Government had given him for his Monastery in Rangoon! Of course, I pointed out that the King's grant was a free gift and not a mere exchange, but that I had heard from General Fytche that morning that the King's agent wanted twenty acres in cantonments, and that the plot required would include the rifle butts and the commissariat and elephant sheds, and that the amount granted by the Government to the King of Burma was more than twice that granted to the King of Siam for similar purposes. The King said that he was not to be compared with the King of Siam !

The Buddhist monks are still afraid to come to see me, but I still go out to them in the evenings and talk with them, and I have given away a large number of books and tracts. I am enabled to place a complete copy of the

Bible in Burmese in sixty of the largest monasteries in Mandalay.

There is not work enough in our small school of fifty or sixty in attendance for so large a staff. With myself, a schoolmaster by nature, it would be desirable to send Mr. Powell to Maulmein.

|Your faithful Servant,

J. E. MARKS.

LETTER 10

To Mr. Jones, Merchant, Rangoon.

Mandalay, April 27th, 1871.

MY DEAR JONES,

To-day, by H.M.'s own request, I wrote him a private letter on the growls of Englishmen against H.M., and the way to satisfy them. I deprecated his nomination of so many royal agents, which I assured him was not for his interest. I suggested that such as you, men of capital and energy, should be called first-class agents, and that there should be agents of the second and third class. I will tell you the result as soon as I know. I have already taken steps in the matter of the *Tsalwè*, and believe that there will be no difficulty in getting the extra three strings.

When I was with H.M. on Tuesday last, Dr. W. was showing drawings, etc., from engines and carriages, for a railway from Mandalay to Toungoo. I believe he is trying to negotiate a loan of some lacs, and I shall strongly urge H.M. not to accept.

Trade seems improving and confidence is gradually being restored.

Yours ever sincerely,

J. E. MARKS.

LETTER II

Mandalay, May 5th, 1871.

To F. W. Rhys Davids, Esq., C.C.S.

I am ashamed to have kept you so long, but, as mentioned before, this is not the region of rapid action, and I am afraid that I am becoming infected with the *genius loci*.

Yesterday I took advantage of an opportunity, when I was alone with the King, to mention your wants. H.M. at once bade me write and tell you that he will be happy to supply you with a copy, not alone of the Dipa Vansa, but of the whole nine books of the series, and that he will forward them through me at an early date.

May I ask if a key to the Burmese characters in which the Pali is written would be of use to you ? If so, I will send you one that I drew up some time ago to accompany the MSS. which I sent home to England.

Believe me, yours sincerely,

J. E. MARKS.

LETTER 12

To J. Talboys Wheeler, Esq.

Mandalay, May 29th, 1871.

In a previous letter to you some time ago I mentioned that while H.M. himself did not hate Major Sladen, or care about his return to Mandalay, H.M.'s Ministers could not work with Major Sladen. To-day, repeating this,

APPENDIX

H.M. informs me that I quite misunderstood his remark. That H.M. has himself the strongest possible objection to Major Sladen's return as Political Agent, if only on the grounds before mentioned, viz, that his Ministers cannot get on with him. The King asked me to let this correction of the meaning of his remark be sent everywhere I had sent my former statement.

Yours most truly,
J. E. MARKS.

LETTER 13

To the Rev. F. R. Vallings.

Mandalay, June 24th, 1871.

MY DEAR VALLINGS,

All is going on fairly here. We have our trials. The King got terribly out of temper with me one day when he heard that Sladen was returning to Mandalay, and threatened to turn me out of the country unless I promised to write to the Government against him. Of course I refused, and there was a small scene. But it was soon over. H.M. made love to me hard, showed more kindness than ever, and respects me, I am sure, more than ever for refusing to deceive him.

Can you count on the S.P.C.K.'s help with a revision of the Burmese Prayer Book ? The first edition is now out of print, and we want now to issue the Litany, Confirmation, Marriage and Baptism service.

The water is rising, and we shall soon be inundated, but we are better prepared. The church gets on well. I have now a goodly number of communicants.

Heartily yours,

J. E. Marks.

LETTER 14

To J. Talboys Wheeler, Esq.

Mandalay, July 11th, 1871.

My dear Wheeler,

You may not be aware that Sladen is one of my best friends ; that it was through him, mainly, if not entirely, that this Mission

278

was started, and that I came to Mandalay.
When he left, his enemies, unofficial as I am,
began to slander him, especially to the King.
On my return from Rangoon in November,
1869, the King at my first interview repeated
some of these slanders as truths. I replied
that I knew them to be false. Whereupon he
waxed wrath and left the room. A month
after, when I was present, the *Yaw atwin wun*
related to H.M. the same tales, whereupon I
rebuked him sharply. The King laughed this
time and said that I was bad tempered, but
that we would talk of something else.

For a year and nine months Sladen's name
was not mentioned to me by H.M. until one
day when he was speaking of his universal
benevolence, how he loved English, French,
Chinese, etc.; he wound up by saying: " And
I do not hate Sladen. It was only my Ministers
who could not get on with him." All believed
that H.M. was opening the door of reconcilia-
tion should Sladen return. I gladly wrote
this to you, Fytche, Sladen and others, but
to none officially, of course.

I certainly must be acquitted of all desire to
interfere in politics. Ever since McMahon's

unwise attempt to make the Burmese Government look upon me as his subordinate, I have zealously tried to convince the King that I have no connection with the Government of India. The Bishop wrote to me : " It will be better that you should be free from Residential authority, except what due friendliness and patriotism may require." You assure me, and I feel that you do so kindly, that my position would be seriously imperilled if it were known or supposed that I discussed the merits of political officers with the King. So then, in the same spirit, I would reply that I do not do so.

My position here is no enviable one, but it is one from which I cannot be relieved. The King threatens to burn the school if I leave, and the Bishop, to whom I had applied for relief, wrote me, in his last letter : " You must stick to your post at all hazard."

Sincerely yours,

J. E. MARKS.

APPENDIX

LETTER 15

To the Sec., S.P.G.

Mandalay, October 2nd, 1871.

The Burma Bible and Tract Society furnished me with a very large supply of books and tracts in Burmese. I have distributed them from time to time, but within the last week or so our compound has been thronged with people going to see the gold-covered and jewel-decked umbrella, or *Hti*, which at enormous expense has been prepared here, and is now on its way down to Rangoon, where it is to crown the Shwé Dagôn pagoda. The *Hti* has cost, I believe, about £25,000.

As soon as it became known that I had tracts to distribute, I was simply besieged for them. All day long people came, and in such numbers that I was obliged to take measures to prevent accidents. Yesterday—Sunday—

my stock began to show signs of exhaustion. A little tract called " Justice and Mercy Reconciled " had been in great demand, and I was reduced to a single copy. So I made all applicants, about three hundred, sit down under our covered way, and read it aloud to them all. I then gave the tract to a venerable old man who had been an earnest listener.

To-day I gave away my last tract and hundreds of applicants have been sent empty away. I would not overrate the importance of the distribution ; but I think there is cause for thankfulness that in Mandalay I should be permitted to distribute thousands of Christian tracts, and that I should find thousands glad and anxious to receive them.

LETTER 16

To the Sec., S.P.G.

Mandalay, October, 1872.

My opportunities for Mission work are here very restricted. I believe that to attempt bazaar preaching would cause such a disturbance as would endanger any prospect of other usefulness in Mandalay. I cannot hide from myself that even our present efforts are regarded with more toleration than favour by the *Hpôngyis* and nobles, and it is only the powerful support of the King which enables us to stand our ground.

I embrace every opportunity of visits from *Hpôngyis* and people to explain the truths of the Gospel. A short time ago one of the *Mingyis* came here with a large retinue. I gave him a copy of the Bible in Burmese which he read eagerly and accepted thankfully, and by his permission I distributed suitable tracts to all his followers. I have a great number of visitors of all ranks. The roads are so bad that the people gladly come through our compound on their way to and from the cemetery. They have always full permission to come into my house and look round, and then they gladly enter into religious conversation and accept Christian tracts and books. Yet even this has aroused considerable excitement, and more than one undoubted friend of the Mission has advised caution in the work.

I have been in close connection with His Majesty since I took up teaching the princes in the Palace. His Majesty always listened kindly and attentively when I talked of our holy religion, and he delighted to tell me of his own religion and of his early life. The young princes were making good progress, and a sixth was sent to join them. But at the end of April all this changed.

I felt very poorly, and determined to take a short trip on the river. I left on the 3rd of May and returned on the 9th. On the day that I left, I heard the news of the death of the *Myouk nan ma daw*, the favourite Queen. His Majesty took this grief much to heart, seeking privacy, and shunning all but absolutely necessary business Since that time I have seen the King but seldom, and only once in private.

I heartily wish that it were in my power to tell you of more material and visible success in our work. But even if it is not given to us to record numerous conversions and baptisms, it is still matter for thankfulness that we may go on giving Christian instruction to nearly a hundred boys and young men, that we may distribute Christian books and tracts, and that we may hold services for the small band of Europeans and native Christians, without let or hindrance.

LETTER 17

To the Sec., S.P.G.

Mandalay, July 23rd, 1874.

REVEREND SIR,

I feel that the time has arrived when it would be vain to hope further that the King will pay the money which he owed when he ceased to support the school, and that I must now look to the Society for that help.

We may not hide it from ourselves any longer that the work of the Mission in the future will have to be carried on, not with the aid of the King, but in spite of him. But, speaking for myself, I cannot say that I regret this. Those who come to us will be more in earnest, and less actuated by worldly motives, while for myself, I cannot but rejoice at the termination of my connection with the Palace, and that I have not to spend day after day waiting for an interview with the King and in application for money for the school and church.

I would not appear too urgent, but I would beg to remind the Society that I am personally responsible for the money. Of course, should the King feel it his duty to pay the back money, and I should be at liberty to accept it, I should at once forward it to you. But there is little likelihood of this, for H.M., to use a homely proverb, is killing the goose that lays the golden eggs of commerce and self-reliance among his people, and of course his treasury is in a chronic state of emptiness.

I do not think that the school in Mandalay can be carried on for less than Rs. 350 per month. It is useless, at present, to think of school fees. It is not Mandalay custom, and we should empty the school if we attempted just now to enforce them.

If the Bishop would sanction an appeal to the public, I will submit a draft for his Lordship's approval. I believe it would tide us over till I get to England, when, if my legs will carry me, I believe I shall be able to get substantial help.

I am, dear Sir,

Your faithful Servant,

J. E. MARKS.

LETTER 18

To Bishop Milman.

Mandalay, October 16th, 1874.

MY LORD BISHOP,

Your kind letter of September 19th reached me on the 12th. I beg to express my most sincere thanks for the kind tone of your Lordship's letter, as well as for your noble letter on my behalf to the Governor-General.

I must confess my intense surprise at the action of the Governor-General in this matter. From what I had heard of Lord Northbrook, I certainly expected very different treatment. That he should withdraw the subsidy for the maintenance " of state services," as the official letter put it, was of course within Government power, and this action was known to the King at least on the same day as it was known to me, and H M publicly interpreted it to mean that the English Government concurred with his conduct towards me.

Lord Northbrook is perhaps not aware that I was sent up here in 1868 by your Lordship, with the full consent of Sir John Lawrence, at the recommendation of General Fytche, who had known me since 1860, and at the particular invitation of H.M.

That the King not only asked your Lordship in 1873 not to send another clergyman here instead of me, but so late as December last, when I had made all arrangements to go home on medical leave, and a *locum tenens* was already in Rangoon, the King asked me, as a personal favour, to postpone my departure for a year, and I did so.

I can only recollect two or three instances in which my conduct here has not met with your Lordship's entire approbation, or has been the subject of correspondence with Government.

The King has been exceedingly angry at my repeated and determined refusal to write his wishes to the Governor-General.

APPENDIX

I would venture to remark that even if on either of the above occasions my conduct was blameworthy, it was the reverse of offence against the Burmese Government.

It has ever been my wish to abstain from interference in politics or business. But this has been exceedingly difficult. The King has ever been accustomed for clergymen to take part in these matters. At the present day the monks are the virtual rulers of the country. In the embassy of Colonel Phayre he had the assistance of the Very Rev. P. Abbona, and H.M. Government of India made a suitable verbal and pecuniary acknowledgment of his aid.

In an interview with the King in the early part of the year, he complained that although he had done so much for me, I had been of no use to him Whilst the Roman Catholic clergy worked for his interest with the Italian and French embassies, H.M. could not understand the abstention from politics on my part.

I cannot accept the entire responsibility of the publication of my reports. Some of these have been published against my wish. I venture to submit that it is my duty to write my reports truthfully, plainly and fearlessly, to give facts and my impressions. The responsibility of publishing these reports must rest with those to whom they are addressed.

I am perfectly willing to accept all responsibility for every one of the facts in my published reports. I challenge the fullest inquiry. That which I reported to the Bible Society a year ago is perfectly true now. I frequently distribute hundreds of tracts in a day. I gave away more than two hundred in my own house the day before yesterday. The matter with the King is simply one of money, and he seized the occasion of that report, misrepresented to him, to try to avoid the payments which had fallen into arrears.

Since April 10th, the day on which the King told me to leave his country, H.M. has not paid the arrears for which Captain Strover twice asked him, but neither have I feared or suffered the least annoyance, injury or insult. I still have no door to my house nor closed gate to my compound. The princes, my former pupils, keep up intercourse with me, and from the heir-apparent, the Thagara Prince, I have this week received very kind and friendly communications. The monks visit us more frequently and in greater numbers than ever.

Mr. Eden wrote to me his belief that when the King ceased to fear that we should trouble him for money, he would be glad to listen to me again, and your Lordship said the same. In a country where the confidential minister of to-day is in prison to-morrow (as I have seen), who can expect always to be in favour ? Your Lordship will not forget how that the King was wishing to ask you to request the Governor-General to remove Captain Strover, who was then out of favour. For my own part, as I informed your Lordship in a previous letter, I will not leave Mandalay until matters are settled by those whose duty it is to decide. I am just now in a very bad state of health and am in the doctor's hands ; but were I much worse and much poorer, I should still feel it my duty to adhere to my resolve. When I can honourably leave Mandalay, nothing would delight me better than to resume the work which ten years ago I commenced in Rangoon.

Your lordship's faithful Servant,

J. E. MARKS.

LETTER 19

To the Sec., S.P.G.

Mandalay, October 30th, 1874.

MY DEAR MR. BRAY,

My telegram, sent with the full consent of Captain Strover, will have informed you that that gentleman has consented to audit the accounts of this Mission, and has certified to their correctness. The result has not been arrived at without considerable trouble to Captain Strover, due, I am afraid, chiefly from my method, or rather want of method, in the keeping of my accounts. We began here in a hand-to-mouth method, and I fear that we have kept to it. But yet all items of receipts and expenditure have been entered, though not all in the same book. This has given Captain Strover so much trouble in balancing all, and I fear that though he has satisfied himself with the correctness of my accounts, he has formed a very poor opinion of my abilities as a book-keeper. This is what has always troubled me in my work more than anything else, and I will certainly ask you to allow me to be relieved of it in Rangoon.

I have written to my successor my view as to what would be advisable for him to do here, and I may say that those views have been endorsed by Captain Strover. I say this: Be friendly with, if possible, but by all means be independent of the King. Never ask him for money. Never receive any without, as the Bishop directed me, sending it to the secretary at Calcutta. So long as he does not ask him for money, H.M. will love and respect him. But if once, induced by royal promises and temporary favour, he becomes involved in a large boarding school or costly day school, he will sooner or later have to " eat dirt."

To-morrow I take my last journey to Bhamo. The kindness of the Company allows me to take sixteen boys free of cost.

Believe me, ever sincerely yours,

J. E. MARKS.

LETTER 20

To the Sec., S.P.G.

St. John's College.
January 23rd, 1875.

You cannot tell how pleased I am to be in
Rangoon again, and how pleased everybody is
to see me. I am holding levees of my boys of
many generations back daily, and the school
is mounting up. It and the Mission will
require all my energies. We have a palatial
High School to do battle with, but I have no
fear. I am really sorry to think of leaving a
work which seems to need me so much. I
cannot yet say definitely whether I can leave
it at all. It depends on other matters.

APPENDIX

LETTER 21

Dr. Marks to King Thibaw on his Accession.
[*Translation.*]

The English Priest salutes the King.

The Priest has heard with much sorrow of the death of the royal father from whom he received many and great gifts for his schools, his pupils and himself.

But the Priest is very glad that your Majesty his royal pupil (*tabyidaw*) has been chosen to reign, and he prays that you may have a long and prosperous reign filled with the blessings of peace and plenty, and that your subjects may be under your rule, numerous, happy, loyal and contented.

The Priest wishes that like your royal father, your Majesty may be famous for your mercy and kindness to all your subjects, and especially he would ask your royal kindness and clemency for the princes, your royal brothers and schoolfellows; that as it is known in England and other countries that your Majesty learned in an English school, so it may be known that when you ascended the throne, your first act was to show mercy and kindness. So all nations will praise you, and know how great and firm your government is.

The Priest has now much work. His school contains 550 boys, with more than 120 boarders. He cannot leave this just now; but in about three months' time he hopes to be able to come to Mandalay to see the power and dignity of his royal pupil.

LETTER 22

Dr. Williams to Dr. Marks (referring to the above letter).

October 24th, 1878.

MY DEAR MR. MARKS,

I duly received your letter for the King, with your note of the 12th. I did not expect that Mr. Shaw would exactly approve.

APPENDIX

The very fact of your showing it to the Chief
Commissioner and the Resident tends to lend
it that character which the official mind not
unnaturally dislikes. Officials do not care
what is said or done by a total outsider, as an
outsider, but if there is the slightest chance of
a communication being regarded as somehow
emanating from, or permitted by, the officials
of Government, those officials become responsible in a measure for the tone as well as the
meaning of the letter.

I have no doubt that the English version
was all that could be desired, but the Burmese
is not perfect. The object of the letter is,
of course, what all sympathize with. I showed
the letter to the S. Byu, who evidently did not
like it. As to presenting it without the sanction of the Wungyis, that is of course out of
the question.

The young King is not a king in the sense
that his father was. The object of the letter
is, I am glad to say, not urgent just now, and
I am sorry to say that your *tabyidaw* is not
showing a docile disposition, and I am myself
afraid that he would resent the letter. You
spoke of the young fellow as determined;

that is the goody word for obstinate. He has
been playing the fool worse and worse, has
begun to speak slightingly of the Ministers, and
has opened his mouth unequivocally as to
the *kalas*. The *Hpôngyis*, too, don't come off
better. He says he *knows them!*

The insecurity of the present state of things
is considerable. The feeling of the people is
that the Ministers have been clever in making
a puppet, but the puppet is turning out a very
ungovernable " human boy " with a strong
touch of the devil in him. I suppose he is
clever in learning by rote, but he certainly
looks a stubborn, sly, unsympathetic lad, and
he always has worn that look since I have
known him.

The princes in prison are all safe and well ;
those at the Residency are safer and better.
Of course, peace is assured, and a new regime
has begun on *parabike*. But the real feeling
in the majority of the men in power is one of
more dislike to the English than in the old
King's time. As to your young Linban Prince
returning here under guarantee, it would be a
piece of folly on his part, and certain cruelty on
the part of those that persuaded him to do so.

APPENDIX

If the Kinwun Mingyi approves of your letter, it will be presented, but I expect it will be, *ma to thay bu*. Wait a little.

Yours sincerely,
C. B. WILLIAMS.

LETTER 23

Sir Charles Aitchison to Dr. Marks.

Government House, Rangoon.
February 13th, 1879.

MY DEAR MR. MARKS,

In this and in all similar matters there is really only one answer I can give. The Government have a representative at Mandalay who has a very ticklish game to play. I cannot say what use the King or his Ministers may make of a private correspondence with you, however harmless that correspondence may be in itself.

It is quite possible that a bad use may be made of it to the embarrassment of Mr. Shaw, and, therefore, when my opinion is asked, I can only advise that nothing should be done of which Mr. Shaw is not fully informed. The case would be very different if the Mandalay Court were less barbarous.

Yours very sincerely,

C. AITCHISON.

THE END

INDEX

INDEX

INDEX

INDEX

INDEX

INDEX